CREATION AND CRITICISM
A Passage to India

CREATION AND CRITICISM

A Passage to India

JUNE PERRY LEVINE

UNIVERSITY OF NEBRASKA PRESS · LINCOLN

Chapter 3 first appeared in somewhat different form as "An Analysis of the Manuscripts of *A Passage to India*" in *PMLA* LXXXV (March 1970). Acknowledgments for the use of copyrighted material appear on pages xi–xii, which constitute an extension of the copyright page.

Publishers on the Plains

UNP

Manufactured in the United States of America

For David

Contents

Preface

MY MAIN PURPOSE in this book is to make Forster's great novel, *A Passage to India*, as accessible as possible to those of its readers who find that their familiarity with Hindu philosophy or Moslem poetry or British dominion over India or other aspects of the work falls short of their wishes. I have also tried to chronicle some of the events of Forster's life that were transformed into his novel—the transforming itself being a mystery beyond chronicling—and to record the critical interpretations of various readers, including myself.

The Introduction offers a brief sketch of Forster's background and ideas up until the publication of *A Passage to India:* who the man was and the tradition he moved within and against. The problem of how an artist uses the raw material of his experiences, which focuses the second chapter, is attacked by comparing biographical data with corresponding portions of the novel. The third chapter pursues the history of the novel's creation by comparisons of a different sort when the manuscript revisions are analyzed. The last two chapters are devoted to criticism: a compendium of Forster studies up until the inception of this book and a reading by the present author.

My method has been to rely on Forster as the best possible source of information—not only his own writings, but those books and articles he refers to. Thus I have mined the Indian travel books of his friends G. L. Dickinson and J. R. Ackerley, the hitherto ignored Indian reportage of Sir Valentine Chirol, the Sufi poems of Jalal-ud-din Rumi, the Hindu gospel of Sri Ramakrishna, and the lore of the Vishnu Purana. And, as I indicated, I have made extensive use of the only recently available manuscript of the novel.

The vicissitudes of manuscripts are often stories in themselves. In the present case, the theft of the first copy and carbon of my work from a garaged automobile led to a year of duplicated efforts and a widened gap between the completion of the research and the publication of the book. Conversely, books yet to appear will have to consider the new material being made available as a result of Forster's death.

I would like to thank Mrs. Leona Mason and Mrs. Charity E. Greene of Love Memorial Library at the University of Nebraska and Mrs. Ann Bowden and Mrs. Frances H. Hudspeth of the Humanities Research Center of the University of Texas for their assistance during the preparation of this manuscript. I also wish to express my gratitude to Professor Walter Wright of the University of Nebraska for his wise counsel, as well as to my colleagues Professor James Roberts and Professor Lee Lemon, who made useful suggestions about the manuscript. Finally, I owe a debt of appreciation to my husband for his help with both the practical concerns and the pondering of ideas during the long time this book has been in the making.

JUNE PERRY LEVINE

University of Nebraska

Acknowledgments

Thanks are due the following publishers for permission to use copyrighted material:

Edward Arnold (Publishers) Ltd. and Harcourt Brace Jovanovich, Inc. for permission to reprint excerpts from the following works by E. M. Forster: *The Hill of Devi*, *Two Cheers for Democracy*, *Marianne Thornton: A Domestic Biography*, and *Abinger Harvest*.

Random House, Inc. for permission to quote from *The Longest Journey* by E. M. Forster, Vintage Books, Random House, Inc., 1962, copyright © 1962 by Random House.

Routledge & Kegan Paul Ltd. and Chilmark Press for permission to quote from "The One Orderly Product" by Frank Kermode in his *Puzzles and Epiphanies: Essays and Reviews, 1958–61*, published in the United States under the title "Mr. E. M. Forster as a Symbolist" in *Forster: A Collection of Critical Essays*, edited by Malcolm Bradbury.

John Murray (Publishers) Ltd. for permission to quote from *Hafiz of Shiraz*, translated by Peter Avery and John Heath-Stubbs, in the "Wisdom of the East" series, published by John Murray Ltd.; and for permission to quote from *The Persian Mystics: Jalalu'd-Din Rumi* by F. Hadland Davis.

Macmillan London and Basingstoke for permission to quote from *Indian Unrest* by Valentine Chirol.

Orient Longmans Ltd. for permission to quote from *Bihar: The Heart of India* by Sir John Houlton, Bombay: Orient Longmans, 1949.

Withers & Company, acting for the Personal Representatives of the late G. Lowes Dickinson, for permission to quote from *Appearances* by G. Lowes Dickinson.

Cornell University Press for permission to quote from *The Novels of E. M. Forster* by James McConkey. © 1957 by Cornell University. Used by permission of Cornell University Press.

New York University Press and Peter Owen Limited for permission to quote from *Art and Order: A Study of E. M. Forster* by Alan Wilde, published in the British Commonwealth by Peter Owen.

Oxford University Press for permission to quote from *Islam in India* by Ja'far Sharif, translated by G. A. Herklots, new edition by William Crooke. Published by Oxford University Press.

Princeton University Press for permission to quote from *E. M. Forster: The Perils of Humanism* by Frederick C. Crews, copyright © 1962 by Princeton University Press; Princeton Paperback 1967. Reprinted by permission of Princeton University Press and Oxford University Press. Also for permission to quote from *The Collected Works of C. G. Jung*, edited by G. Adler, M. Fordham, and H. Read, translated by R. F. C. Hull, Bollingen Series XX, volume 9i, *The Archetypes and the Collective Unconscious*, copyright ©

1959 and 1969 by the Bollingen Foundation, Princeton University Press.

Routledge & Kegan Paul Ltd., publishers of *The Collected Works of C. G. Jung* in the United Kingdom and British Commonwealth (excluding Canada).

Stanford University Press for permission to quote from *The Cave and the Mountain: A Study of E. M. Forster* by Wilfred Stone. Copyright © 1966 by Stanford University Press.

University of Toronto Press for permission to quote from *Rhythm in the Novel* by E. K. Brown, copyright, Canada, 1950 by University of Toronto Press; and for permission to quote from Hugh Maclean, "The Structure of the Novel," *University of Toronto Quarterly* XXII (January, 1953).

CREATION AND CRITICISM
A Passage to India

1. Introduction

WRITING OF HIS VISIT in 1921 to a small Indian Native State, Dewas Senior, E. M. Forster was to say thirty-two years later, "It was the great opportunity of my life."[1] He never ascribed to any other experience, not even the undergraduate years at his beloved Cambridge, such importance. All that had gone before—a childhood spent in the English countryside; an explorative career at the university; previous travels in Greece, Italy, India, and Egypt; his notion that an Indian temple might reveal the Truth—had prepared him to make this sojourn the central event of his long life and the impetus for his greatest book, *A Passage to India* (1924). As he wrote in his second novel, "There comes a moment—God knows when—at which we can say, 'I will experience no longer. I will create. I will be an experience.'"[2]

Forster did not merely recognize his opportunity when it arose. He dared it and rode it to the source. His masterwork charts his passage to India and, for generations of

1. E. M. Forster, *The Hill of Devi* (New York: Harcourt, Brace & Co., 1953), p. 8.

2. E. M. Forster, *The Longest Journey* (New York: Random House, Vintage Books, 1962), p. 66. First published in 1907.

readers, it has encompassed, as well, the essential Western experience of the East: attempted political dominion combined with a feeling of racial superiority, dissatisfaction with the limits of empirical rationalism countered by an uneasy attraction to a mysticism that heals or confounds.

Although he did not publish another novel during the forty-six years that remained to him, Forster's reputation is today undiminished; his achievement unassailed. New biographical material may emerge and perhaps also the frequently mentioned "locked away" novel, but we already know enough about the man, his times, and his subject to be able to understand the book which exists at the intersection of these three arcs: what he put into it and why it holds us still.

The salient facts of Edward Morgan Forster's life have often been recorded. An only child, he was born in 1879. At Cambridge he was asked to join the famed "Apostles" whose membership at that time included Leonard Woolf, Maynard Keynes, Lytton Strachey, and Desmond Mac-Carthy. Friendships among the "Apostles" helped form the Bloomsbury group, with whom Forster was also intimate. He began writing early—both essays and fiction—and between 1902 and 1911 published four novels and a collection of stories. The appearance of *A Passage to India* secured his reputation. Asked to deliver the Clark Lectures at Cambridge in 1927, he presented the critical treatise published later that year as *Aspects of the Novel*. Forster returned to King's in his later years as an honorary fellow of the college. He died in June, 1970.

Until there is a full-length biography of Forster, detailed knowledge about him can best be gathered from the wide range of his writings, chief among them the biography of his great-aunt, Marianne Thornton. Forster considered family stock of importance and the strains which met in him interested him a good deal. One discovers two rather different heritages. Emphasis has usually been given to his father's mother's family, the highly respected Thorntons of Clapham Common; less has been made of his mother's family, the Whichelos, who were of humbler stock and achievement; his paternal grandmother's father had been a wealthy banker and M.P., his maternal grandmother's husband a drawing master who died leaving a poor widow with ten children. Yet of his mother's mother, and of his mother's side, he writes, "it is with her—with them—that my heart lies." [3] The Whichelos were gay, improvident, artistic, and likable. Forster's "refusal to be great," his mistrust of pomp and religiosity, his irony and light touch—all this is in the Whichelo manner. The Thorntons were pious, rich, sensible, and impressive. Forster recognized the worthiness of his father's family, but remained detached enough to be critical. Writing of the weakness of the "Thornton-Wilberforce outlook" which opposed slavery abroad, but ignored the need for domestic reform, he says:

> When slavery was industrial they did nothing and had no thought of doing anything; they regarded it as something "natural," to encounter it was an educational experience, and an opportunity for smug thankfulness. Misery might be alleviated at the soup-kitchen level, but to do more might make the workers unruly and even un-Christian. Hence Hannah Moore's tracts, recommending industry, frugality, obedience, and harder and still harder work. Hence Wilberforce's unsatisfactory record in Parliament when it came to Home Affairs—his

3. E. M. Forster, *Marianne Thornton: A Domestic Biography* (New York: Harcourt, Brace & Co., 1956), p. 279. Neither Forster nor his critics have offered much information about his paternal grandfather's family. The Reverend Charles Forster came of poor, Irish gentlefolk.

support of the Combination Acts, his approval of the
Peterloo massacre—and hence Francis Place's description
of him as "an ugly epitome of the devil."

I agree with the above line of criticism. But I do not
share the moral indignation that sometimes accompanies
it. The really bad people, it seems to me, are those who
do no good anywhere and help no one either at home or
abroad. There are plenty of them about, and when they
are clever as well as selfish they often manage to slip
through their lives unnoticed, and so escape the censure
of historians.[4]

According to Forster's values, there is an even more
crucial weakness in the Thornton philosophy, and "indifference to the unseen" which strikes their descendant
as "the great defect in my great-grandfather's set, and the
reason why they have not made a bigger name in history."[5]
The limitation of rationalism is, of course, a major theme
in Forster's fiction, including *A Passage to India*.

Despite these reservations, Forster's attitude toward his
forebears was notably affectionate. Some critics claim to
have found in him hostility, conscious or unconscious,
toward his father, who died when Forster was not quite
two years old, thus "abandoning" him in the world.[6] But
the little that Forster has written about his father is
marked by candor rather than anger: "He was quick at
the uptake, amusing, sarcastic, could always make old
Monie [Marianne Thornton] laugh, and he had integrity
and unselfishness. How these qualities combined to make
him a real person I do not know. He has always remained
remote to me. I have never seen myself in him, and the

4. Ibid., pp. 48–49.
5. E. M. Forster, "Henry Thornton," in *Two Cheers for Democracy* (New
York: Harcourt, Brace & Co., Harvest Books, 1951), p. 195. This essay
first appeared in 1939.
6. Wilfred Stone in *The Cave and the Mountain* (Stanford, Calif.: Stanford
University Press, 1966) is the chief proponent of this psychoanalytic
viewpoint.

letters from him and the photographs of him have not helped." [7] Aside from the autobiographical interest of this passage, it is helpful in understanding Forster's ideas about a "real" person and, by extension, a "real" character. "Qualities" are of limited usefulness in envisioning someone; it is how they "combine" that is essential. The combinations create the complexity and ambiguity of behavior.

Many of his readers have heard of the new world that Cambridge opened to Forster when he entered King's College after an unhappy time at public school as a Tonbridge day-boy.[8] "That the public school is not infinite and eternal, that there is something more compelling in life than team-work and more vital than cricket, that firmness, self-complacency and fatuity do not between them compose the whole armour of man," [9]—this is what Forster discovered at Cambridge. The standard-bearers of the public school ethos, paragons of "firmness, self-complacency and fatuity"—like Ronnie Heaslop in *A Passage to India*—are always the target of sharp attack. Rickie Elliot in *The Longest Journey* follows his creator's path at the university: "He had crept cold and friendless and ignorant out of a great public school, preparing for a silent and solitary journey, and praying as a highest favour that he might be left alone. Cambridge had not answered his prayer. She had taken and soothed him, and warmed him, and had laughed at him a little, saying that he must not be so tragic yet awhile, for his boyhood had been but a dusty corridor that led to the spacious halls of youth" (p. 4).

Forster delighted in Cambridge because it satisfied his

7. Forster, *Marianne Thornton*, p. 235.

8. Lionel Trilling, *E. M. Forster* (New York: New Directions, 1943), pp. 26–27.

9. E. M. Forster, *Goldsworthy Lowes Dickinson* (New York: Harcourt, Brace & Co., 1934), p. 26.

need to "connect." He wrote in *Howards End*, "Only connect the prose and the passion, and both will be exalted, and human love will be seen at its height. Live in fragments no longer. Only connect, and the beast and the monk, robbed of the isolation that is life to either, will die." [10] And of Cambridge, he wrote, "Body and spirit, reason and emotion, work and play, architecture and scenery, laughter and seriousness, life and art—these pairs which are elsewhere contrasted were there fused into one. People and books reinforced one another, intelligence joined hands with affection, speculation became a passion, and discussion was made profound by love." [11] In 1941, he called Cambridge, simply, "the place which I have loved for forty years, and where I have made my best friends." [12]

An eight-thousand-pound bequest from his great-aunt, Marianne Thornton, made possible Forster's attendance at the university. The bequest was, he said, the "financial salvation" of his life:

> Thanks to it, I was able to go to Cambridge—impossible otherwise, for I failed to win scholarships. After Cambridge I was able to travel for a couple of years, and travelling inclined me to write. After my first visit to India and after the First World War the value of the £8,000 began to diminish, and later on it practically vanished. But by then my writings had begun to sell, and I have been able to live on them instead. [13]

Forster was a professional writer attempting to earn his living in an area the Edwardians called belles-lettres. He was more prolific than has usually been acknowledged.

10. E. M. Forster, *Howards End* (New York: Random House, Vintage Books, 1954), p. 187. First published in 1910.

11. Forster, *Dickinson*, p. 35.

12. Forster, "Cambridge," in *Two Cheers for Democracy*, p. 348. This essay first appeared in 1941.

13. Forster, *Marianne Thornton*, pp. 324–25.

The periodicals he wrote for most frequently between the first Indian trip and *A Passage to India* are the *New Weekly*, the *Daily News*, the *Daily News and Leader*, the *Athenaeum*, and the *Nation and Athenaeum*. In 1920, he was literary editor of the *Daily Herald*, a liberal weekly. In that and the previous year together, he published eighty-eight articles. He was also busy with some abortive projects: an unpublished play, *The Heart of Bosnia* (1911); *Arctic Summer* (a novel begun before *Howards End*); an untitled novel, about a large family (begun after *Howards End*). His subject matter was various: the arts, history, politics, travel, manners, other cultures—in short, civilization.

From his university days onward, Forster had been a citizen of the world. Ironically, the empire which he deplored provided the opportunity of his life; Britain's imperialism made of even her censorious sons cosmopolitans. The first of his trips abroad took place in 1901 when, after a fourth year at Cambridge, Forster visited Greece and Italy, returning to England in 1902. Greece impressed itself on his art—directly in the employment of pagan gods in his fiction,[14] and indirectly in his use of symbolism—aside from generally influencing his views on beauty and style. In *The Longest Journey*, Mr. Jackson, the humanist schoolmaster, "tries to express all modern life in terms of Greek mythology, because the Greeks looked very straight at things, and Demeter or Aphrodite are thinner veils than 'The survival of the fittest' or 'A marriage has been arranged,' and the other draperies of modern journalese" (p. 189). As for Italy, Forster's own voice sounds in Fielding's thoughts about Venice, when, in *A Passage to India*, he is returning home to England.

14. Consider Phaeton, the carriage driver in *A Room with a View*, as well as the short stories "Other Kingdom," "The Curate's Friend," and "The Story of a Panic," and the conception of Stephen Wonham in *The Longest Journey*.

Venice offers him "the harmony between the works of man and the earth that upholds them, the civilization that has escaped muddle, the spirit in a reasonable form, with flesh and blood subsisting. . . . The Mediterranean is the human norm." [15]

In October of 1912, Forster left Naples for his first Indian visit, traveling with his friends Robert Trevelyan, the poet, and the Cambridge don G. Lowes Dickinson. He stayed until the following spring. [16] Since his 1921 visit began in March and lasted through the autumn, Forster's Indian journeys comprised a calendar year. The sense of a weather cycle is as fundamental to the structure of *A Passage to India* as it is to Thoreau's *Walden*.

During the First World War, Forster came to know Egypt, the country in which he was stationed as the result of his volunteering for the Red Cross. "I arrived there in the autumn of 1915 in a slightly heroic mood," he later wrote. "A Turkish invasion was threatened, and although a civilian I might find myself in the battle line. The threat passed and my mood changed. What had began as an outpost turned into something suspiciously like a funk-hole, and I stuck in it for over three years, visiting hospitals, collecting information, and writing reports." [17] Because of this Egyptian experience, he had, by the time he wrote *A Passage to India*, an especially full knowledge of Islam.

The importance of travel to Forster's scheme of things is illustrated by his later complaints about the altered nature of modern tourism. It "misses the graciousness and the gravity of the earlier travel, the personal approach, the individual adventure, the precious possibilities of

15. E. M. Forster, *A Passage to India* (New York: Harcourt, Brace & Co., 1924), p. 282. All references are to this edition.

16. E. M. Forster, "Indian Entries," *Encounter* XVIII (January 1962), 20.

17. E. M. Forster, *Alexandria: A History and a Guide* (Garden City, N.Y.: Doubleday & Co., Anchor Books, 1961), p. xv. First published in 1922.

friendship between visitor and visited." [18] One of the main reasons for his desiring to revisit India in 1921 was to see his good friend Syed Ross Masood, whose personality, in turn, colored *A Passage to India*.[19] Such adventures and friendships figure largely in the writing he produced between his first published story, "Albergo Empedocle" (1903), and *A Passage to India* (1924). *Where Angels Fear to Tread*, his first novel, published in 1905, presents an attempted rescue of an innocent from the depraved foreign society of Italy by a young man whose background is similar to Forster's—a plot rather like that of Henry James's *The Ambassadors*. In fact, according to Rose Macaulay, Forster's book was first called *Rescue*.[20] His second and fourth novels, *The Longest Journey* (1907) and *Howards End* (1910), are set entirely in England; but the third, *A Room With a View* (1908), which was begun after *Where Angels Fear to Tread* but put aside for *The Longest Journey*, is divided between England and Italy. Of the twelve stories Forster reprinted in collections, "The Road from Colonus" takes place, aside from the epilogue, in Greece, and "The Story of the Siren," "The Eternal Moment," and "The Story of a Panic" are set in Italy. Prior to *A Passage to India*, he also published two works drawn from his Egyptian experiences, *Pharos and Pharillon*, a collection of essays, and *Alexandria: A History and a Guide*.

Forster's travels and his liberalism reinforced each other. *The Celestial Omnibus* (1911), the first collection of stories, is dedicated to the memory of the *Independent Review*, described elsewhere by Forster as "a monthly controlled by an editorial board of friends, who had

18. E. M. Forster, "Tourism v. Thuggism," review of *Portrait of Greece* by Lord Kinross, *Listener* LVII (January 17, 1957), 124.

19. Forster, *The Hill of Devi*, p. 81.

20. Rose Macaulay, *The Writings of E. M. Forster* (New York: Harcourt, Brace & Co., 1938), p. 36.

encouraged me to start writing." [21] Its political commitment was also Forster's. In an oft-quoted paragraph from his biography of G. Lowes Dickinson, he writes that "the main aim of the review was political. It was founded to combat the aggressive Imperialism and the Protection campaign of Joe Chamberlain; and to advocate sanity in foreign affairs and a constructive policy at home. It was not so much a Liberal review as an appeal to Liberalism from the Left to be its better self—one of those appeals which have continued until the extinction of the Liberal Party." [22] Almost all of Forster's early work was published in the *Independent Review*. Two of the men connected with it had been his teachers at King's College, Cambridge: Dickinson and Nathaniel Wedd, of whom the novelist says, "it is to him ... more than to anyone—that I owe such awakening as has befallen me." His obvious admiration for the *Review*'s goals and his affection for its editors color his statement that "the first number lies on the table as I write: as fresh and attractive to hold as when I bought it on a bookshelf at St. Pancras thirty years back, and thought the new age had begun."

"An Edwardian in point of time, ... he is equally so in spirit," according to Frederick C. Crews. [23] Placing himself more elaborately, Forster writes in a 1946 essay:

> I belong to the fag-end of Victorian liberalism, and can look back to an age whose challenges were moderate in their tone, and the cloud on whose horizon was no bigger

21. E. M. Forster, *The Collected Tales of E. M. Forster* (New York: Alfred A. Knopf, 1947), p. viii. This collection comprises the stories published in *The Celestial Omnibus* and *The Eternal Moment*.

22. Forster, *Dickinson*, p. 115. The two quotations following are from the same source, pp. 73 and 116.

23. Frederick C. Crews, *E. M. Forster: The Perils of Humanism* (Princeton, N.J.: Princeton University Press, 1962), p. 3. Copyright © 1962 by Princeton University Press. All quotations from this work reprinted by permission of Princeton University Press and Oxford University Press.

than a man's hand. In many ways it was an admirable
age. It practiced benevolence and philanthropy, was
humane and intellectually curious, upheld free speech,
had little colour-prejudice, believed that individuals are
and should be different, and entertained a sincere faith
in the progress of society. The world was to become
better and better, chiefly through the spread of parlia-
mentary institutions.[24]

Forster, the Edwardian, can also be seen in terms of an
earlier nineteenth-century dichotomy, that between
Bentham, the utilitarian, analyzer, and mechanist; and
Coleridge, the romanticist, synthesist, and organic creator.
This schema puts him squarely in the Coleridgian camp.[25]
In any event, there can be little confusion concerning
Forster's ideas about art, criticism, creativity, govern-
ment, religion, morality, or metaphysics; few authors have
spelled out their credos in such detail. However, since
much of this material was written after the completion of
A Passage to India, it is relevant only when it echoes ideas
which were published *prior* to that novel.

Forster's passionate commitment to art did not come at
the expense of his concern for life. When reading him on
the two domains one is curious to discover how this
paradox has been brought off.

"Creation," he writes, "lies at the heart of civilization
like fire in the heart of earth."[26] This vital energy of the
culture—and for Forster, culture matters; he has faith in
it[27]—manifests itself in art. Chief of art's wonders is that
it orders: it "creates little worlds of its own, possessing
internal harmony, in the bosom of this disordered

24. Forster, "The Challenge of Our Time," in *Two Cheers for Democracy*,
p. 56. This essay first appeared in 1946.
25. Stone, *The Cave and the Mountain*, p. 5.
26. Forster, "Three Anti-Nazi Broadcasts," in *Two Cheers for Democracy*,
p. 43. This essay first appeared in 1940.
27. Forster, "Does Culture Matter?," ibid., p. 101. This essay first
appeared in 1940.

planet."[28] And such a world, "while it lasts, seems more
real and solid than this daily existence of pickpockets and
trams."[29] "It is the world within. And since the poet
cannot hope to escape from this world, he should at all
costs arrange and rule it sensibly."[30] Although it is
"remote from life," art "enhances life's values."[31] One
major aspect in which art differs from life is that art can
possess a quality psychologists call "closure." Writing of
a Schumann piece, Forster says, "The melody rose, un-
profitably magical. It broke; it was resumed broken, not
marching once from the cradle to the grave. The sadness
of the incomplete—the sadness that is often Life, but should
never be Art—throbbed in its disjected phrases, and made
the nerves of the audience throb."[32] Schumann is magical,
but the world he creates does not have the salient feature
of order that Beethoven's has—completion. Two decades
later, however, Forster decided that the ordered world of
the artist did not depend on the principle of finiteness; the
imagination could have greater freedom if the form—"the
outward evidence of order"[33]—possessed the capacity for
further growth: "Expansion. That is the idea the novelist
must cling to. Not completion. Not rounding off but
opening out."[34]

Art bears other gifts to the beholder. It "can solace

28. Forster, "The Challenge of Our Time," p. 59.
29. Forster, "Anonymity: An Enquiry," in *Two Cheers for Democracy*, p.
81. This essay is of special interest because it was first published in 1925—
much earlier than most of the others in the collection.
30. E. M. Forster, "The Poetry of C. P. Cavafy," in *Pharos and Pharillon*
(New York: Alfred A. Knopf, 1962), p. 93. The essay was first published in
1919, the book in 1923.
31. Forster, *Howards End*, p. 88.
32. E. M. Forster, *A Room with a View* (New York: Random House,
Vintage Books, 1960), p. 140. First published in 1908.
33. Forster, "Art for Art's Sake," in *Two Cheers for Democracy*, p. 94. This
essay first appeared in 1949.
34. E. M. Forster, *Aspects of the Novel* (New York: Harcourt, Brace & Co.,
Harvest Books, 1956), p. 169. First published in 1927.

us. . . . [By suggesting] a more comprehensible and thus a more manageable human race, [it gives us] the illusion of perspicacity and power." It can—especially in the form of the modern novel—heighten our sense of the freedom of the will, of the triumph of human intention over the impersonal forces of fate. Forster praises an interesting and sensitive French critic who writes under the name of Alain and who has some helpful if slightly fantastic remarks on this point: "What is fictitious in a novel is not so much the story as the method by which thought develops into action, a method which never occurs in daily life. . . . History, with its emphasis on external causes, is dominated by the notion of fatality, whereas there is no fatality in the novel; there, everything is founded on human nature, and the dominating feeling is of an existence where everything is intentional, even passions and crimes, even misery."[35] Art can also bridge the gap between intellect and feeling which some thinkers consider the greatest schism in the modern world: "Music, like all the arts, is making the double appeal to emotion and thought, and great music so makes it that it seems, while we listen, a single appeal, and only afterward do we realize that two sides of our nature have been involved."[36] But art improves on life only because it is subsumed by life. Dante, who is one of the drivers of "The Celestial Omnibus," tells the pedant who would worship him, "I am the means and not the end. I am the food and not the life."[37] And Forster says of Gibbon, whom he greatly admired, "He loved books but was not dominated by them."[38]

35. Ibid., pp. 64, 46.

36. E. M. Forster, "A Concert of Old Instruments," *Athenaeum*, July 11, 1919, p. 597.

37. Forster, *Collected Tales*, p. 73.

38. Forster, "In My Library," in *Two Cheers for Democracy*, p. 304. In this essay, which first appeared in 1949, Forster says Gibbon is one of the authors

Although Forster declares that "art is not all gossamer ... it has become part of our armour,"[39] he never suggests that the chief uses of art are moral. George Crabbe's "moral values" are "not good enough reason for reading him, or for reading anyone."[40] In any event, "a writer's duty often exceeds any duty he owes to society."[41] If art seems to get the approving nod more often than life, it must be remembered that Forster most admired imagination, tolerance, affection, and honesty—qualities which cut across the two domains.

Forster also held a number of other beliefs which are sometimes considered mutually exclusive. American political parlance would class him as a liberal, yet he had a conservative strain something akin to that of our southern literary agrarian movements like the Fugitives. That is, he gives two cheers for democracy because "it admits variety and ... permits criticism";[42] he was always an enemy of imperialism and an advocate of the broadest liberty for all: a thoroughgoing egalitarian. But he hated our technological society and felt the likeliest place to achieve the "connection" he so desired is on an English farm where, he writes, more likely than in any other place, "one might see life steadily and see it whole,

---

whose books he would want in every room. The other two are Shakespeare and Jane Austen. In "A Book That Influenced Me," a radio script written in 1944 and shortened for the same collection, he rates *The Decline and Fall of the Roman Empire*, *War and Peace*, and *The Divine Comedy* as the three great books of his life.

39. E. M. Forster, "A Note on the Way," in *Abinger Harvest* (New York: Noonday Press, Meridian Books, 1955), p. 71. This essay was first published in 1934.

40. E. M. Forster, "Sidling after Crabbe," review of *The Poetry of Crabbe* by Lillian Haddakin, *Listener* LIII (June 9, 1955), 1039.

41. Forster, "English Prose between 1918 and 1939," in *Two Cheers for Democracy*, p. 274. This essay first appeared in 1944.

42. Forster, "What I Believe," ibid., p. 70. This essay first appeared in 1939.

group in one vision its transitoriness and its eternal youth,
connect—connect without bitterness until all men are
brothers." [43] He knew that industrialism and the welfare
state gradually are emancipating the working man—
whom he liked but did not patronize. Still, everything is
so ugly. There is

> a huge economic movement which has been taking the
> whole world, Great Britain included, from agriculture
> towards industrialism. . . . It has meant organisation and
> plans and the boosting of the community. It has meant
> the destruction of feudalism and relationship based on
> the land, it has meant transference of power from the
> aristocrat to the bureaucrat and the manager and the
> technician. Perhaps it will mean democracy, but it has
> not meant it yet, and personally I hate it. [44]

Since Forster was both a democrat and a nostalgic
traditionalist—"If you drop traditional culture you lose
your chance of connecting work and play and creating a
life which is all of a piece" [45]—he had difficulty with the
role of science. Science does "not bring happiness or
wisdom" but at least it represents the world as its practi-
tioners think it is, not as they think it ought to be. Thus, in
its historic war with Christianity, Forster supports "the
age of enquiry" as against "the age of authority." [46]

Although Forster's heritage was Anglican, he was
neither a Christian nor an atheist and although often
labeled antirationalistic, he has written, "There has
always been mystery, perhaps there should always be
mystery, but it is for the free spirit of man to reduce the
mysteriousness and extend the frontiers of the known." [47]

43. Forster, *Howards End*, p. 269.
44. Forster, "English Prose between 1918 and 1939," p. 273.
45. Forster, "Does Culture Matter?" p. 103.
46. Forster, *Alexandria*, pp. 41, 45.
47. E. M. Forster, "The Legacy of Samuel Butler," *Listener* XLVII (June
12, 1952), 956.

This statement is a fine example of how he often managed to have it both ways. But such a criticism would not disturb him for he believed that "the human mind is not a dignified organ"; he did not see "how we can exercise it sincerely except through eclecticism."[48] As regards the organized Christian churches, however, he is unequivocal: "I think that such influence as [Christianity] retains in modern society is due to the money behind it, rather than to its spiritual appeal. It was a spiritual force once, but the indwelling spirit will have to be restated if it is to calm the waters again, and probably restated in a non-Christian form."[49] Forster's response to various religions of the world will be treated more fully in ensuing chapters, but I hope it is clear so far that his detachment from Christianity does not entail a repudiation of the unseen for the seen: "Our business is not to contrast the two, but to reconcile them."[50]

This unaggressive Edwardian, member of a suspect class in a fading society, who showed his allegiance to that society by caring enough to criticize it, is welcome today for his free and reflective spirit. His mind was weighed down with surprisingly little extra baggage and he was never in a rush to establish any program. *A Passage to India*, his chief work, will surely endure.

48. Forster, *Aspects of the Novel*, p. 147.
49. Forster, "What I Believe," pp. 75–76.
50. Forster, *Howards End*, p. 104. Margaret Schlegel, perhaps the only one of his characters to whom Forster accords unstinting approval, wrote this to her sister Helen.

2. The Raw Material of *A Passage to India*

IN THE MAKING of *A Passage to India*, the raw material Forster had at hand, aside from the ideas he already held and the people he had known before journeying to the subcontinent, was abundant: the tensions aroused by England's domination of India; the overwhelming impact of the land itself on Forster; his study of the richly complicated Moslem and Hindu cultures; the particular events of his two trips—especially his friendship with the Maharajah of Dewas.

In Forster's novel, India may well symbolize the "contemporary condition" of man's alienation as James McConkey, among other critics, has held.[1] But it is the specific circumstance of the English presence in India which informs *A Passage to India*, so that a knowledge of Indian history, possessed by Forster and most other

1. "India is more than a foreign land which the English may leave at their wish: it is the contemporary condition, the separation between all mankind and all earth" (James McConkey, *The Novels of E. M. Forster* [Ithaca, N.Y.: Cornell University Press, 1957], p. 82. © 1957 by Cornell University Press. All quotations from this work used by permission of Cornell University Press.)

Englishmen a half century ago, is necessary for today's reader. The British were a long time in changing their early seventeenth-century trading posts into a nineteenth-century empire and it is doubtful that the conversion would have occurred if the Moslem Empire had not simultaneously been in the process of dissolution. The Moslem conquest of India had required six hundred years from the first plundering expeditions of the eighth century to the total occupation of the country in the fourteenth century.

Throughout India's long, convoluted history, the city of Patna, under a variety of names such as Pataliputra and Bankipore, has been a chief center of civilization. And it is this city which Forster uses as the model for Chandrapore[2]—most probably because in a work one of whose principal features is the condensation and expression of the genius of a country, what better major setting than a place saturated with Indian history? Patna was the capital of the first great empire of India, the Maurya Empire, founded by Chandragupta in the fourth century, B.C. His grandson Asoka, a Buddhist, is the preeminent ruler of Indian history until Akbar appears eighteen hundred years later. And the golden age of Hinduism and classical Sanskrit literature, the Gupta Empire of the fourth and fifth centuries, A.D., again flowers in Patna and the surrounding Province of Bihar: the history and traditions

2. "Chandrapore is suggested geographically by Bankipore but its inhabitants are imaginary" (E. M. Forster's notes to the Everyman's Library edition of *A Passage to India* [London: J. M. Dent & Sons, 1942], p. xxxi). A quarter of a century after Forster wrote of Chandrapore, another writer described Patna thus: "The fine old residences of the Commissioner and other officials in this neighborhood have nearly all been rebuilt since the earthquake [1934] or have fallen into disrepair. The Civil Surgeon's house near the river bank is one of the old buildings which has survived. Passing the administrative offices on our left and the fine open space, the *Maidan*, formerly used for a racecourse, the Bankipore Club buildings are on the river bank near the Anglican Church" (Sir John Houlton, *Bihar: The Heart of India* [Bombay: Orient Longmans, 1949], p. 22).

of this region "go back to the earliest dawn; the relics of its glorious past can still be seen in its ancient cities or once almost forgotten sites; it was the scene of the life's work of the most venerated names in two of the world's great religions —Gautama Buddha and Vardhamma Mahavira—and one of the world's great rulers, the Emperor Asoka." [3]

During the Moslem conquest, Hindu culture stagnated, unable to absorb Islam. This is the period, especially its heyday from 1526 to 1707, to which Forster's Dr. Aziz, himself an ardent Moslem, frequently refers in *A Passage to India* as when he says, "Mr. Fielding, must not India have been beautiful then, with the Mogul Empire at its height and Alamgir reigning at Delhi upon the Peacock Throne?" (p. 66). During the expedition to the Marabar Caves, Aziz discusses the history of Moslem rule with Mrs. Moore and Adela Quested. He tells them that he feels "like the Emperor Babur. . . . Because my ancestors came down with him from Afghanistan. They joined him at Herat. He also had often no more elephants than one, none sometimes, but he never ceased showing hospitality" (p. 143). For Aziz, who finds the British oppressive and the Hindus contemptible, to identify himself with Babur is to recall the rise of triumphant Moslem rule in India. After this praise of Babur—who was descended from Tamerlane on his father's side and from Genghis Khan on his mother's —Adela replies that she thought Aziz's "favourite" emperor was Alamgir, called in English books Aurangzebe. "Alamgir?" Aziz replies. "Oh yes, he was of course the more pious. But Babur—never in his whole life did he betray a friend" (p. 144). Alamgir seems to have been "a stern puritan and religious bigot who persecuted Hindus and everywhere substituted Moslems for Hindus. He ate no animal food and drank only water. He allowed himself no self-indulgence in pleasures, fasted much, and tried

3. Houlton, *Bihar*, p. 1.

to suppress singing and dancing."[4] In his guided tour
through Moslem rule, Aziz turns from the pious Alamgir
to another of the six chief Mogul emperors, Akbar, who
"is very wonderful," but, he admits "half a Hindu; he
was not a true Moslem" (pp. 144–45). According to
authorities, "the reign of Akbar, who was one of the
greatest rulers of India, was marked by firmness and
benevolence and by a policy of toleration and conciliation
of Hindus. . . . He had an enquiring and receptive mind
that tried to understand all creeds and doctrines; he went
so far as to give up Islam and tried unsuccessfully to found
a new eclectic religion."[5] Later, in the "Temple" section
of *A Passage to India*, Forster uses all of this historical
material emblematically, as a figure for Aziz's disavowal
of narrow-mindedness in favor of tolerance: "When Aziz
arrived [at Mau], and found that even Islam was idola-
trous, he grew scornful, and longed to purify the place,
like Alamgir. But soon he didn't mind, like Akbar" (p.
296). Thus, the pantheon of Mogul emperors is arranged as an analogue to the idea of universal love which
"Temple" structures.

Aziz does not forgive the British for ending the Moslem
Empire, but the empire seems to have been doomed by its
own fragmentation. According to the *Encyclopedia Americana*, "European initiative, enterprise, and greed, armed
with powerful European weapons and assisted by Indian
disunity and treachery, completed the destruction of the
Mogul Empire and laid the foundations of British
ascendancy"; according to the *Encyclopaedia Britannica*,
"the gradual decay of the Mogul Empire from within, and
the consequent anarchy, forced the English to take up
arms in their own defence, and triumphing over one
enemy after another they found themselves at last in the

4. *Encyclopedia Americana*, 1956 ed., s.v. "India."
5. Ibid.

place of the Moguls."[6] Whichever version one accepts, the result was the same: the Moslems were supplanted and by 1815 the British Raj was under way.

During the nineteenth century, the British gradually created the machinery of the government of India whose administrative head was the secretary of state for India, a cabinet member, and whose agent in India was the viceroy. An excellent guide to the complexities of Anglo-Indian relations, suggested by Forster himself but hitherto ignored by Forster's scholars, is Sir Valentine Chirol, described in *The Hill of Devi* as "a traveling journalist of repute," and author of *Indian Unrest*.[7] Chirol, whose work first appeared in 1910 in the London *Times* as a series of articles "From Our Special Correspondent in India,"[8] is, not surprisingly, more sanguine about the British role in India than is Forster. However, the *Dictionary of National Biography* estimate seems fair: "An admirer of the great achievements of the British Raj, he was also from the first a sympathizer with the native point of view."[9] Chirol's work is of especial interest, first, because it is clear from *The Hill of Devi* that Forster had read it, in all probability just before his 1912 trip to India, and second, because it was also widely read by other informed Englishmen and helped to shape their opinions shortly before the First World War.

The war changed conditions in India markedly and one of the problems *A Passage to India* presents, because it names no dates, is whether its pages reflect the still largely acquiescent India of Forster's first visit or the aroused India of a decade later. Of course, as is apparent from the

6. Ibid., *Encyclopaedia Britannica*, 11th ed., s.v. "India."

7. Forster, *The Hill of Devi*, pp. 79, 70.

8. The series of articles by Sir Valentine Chirol which began in the *Times* (London) on July 16, 1910, comprised the book *Indian Unrest* (London: Macmillan & Co., 1910).

9. *Dictionary of National Biography*, 1922–30, s.v. "Chirol, Valentine."

title of Chirol's book, unrest in India was not a new phenomenon; it was fostered by nationalism which had been stirring increasingly since before the turn of the century. However, Chirol's major assumption in 1910 was the impossibility of Britain's ever conceding to India the rights of self-government.[10] By the time of *A Passage to India*, the issue is no longer decided; rather, it is raised. And in *Hindu Holiday*, written about 1930, J. R. Ackerley speaks of Indian independence as if it were inevitable.[11]

Ruling India presented enormous problems to the British. One-fifth of the population was Moslem, and Chirol writes that the more the British delegated authority, the more power the Hindu majority would gain at the expense of this minority. As a consequence, the Moslem population became separatist (p. 126). Then again, the Indian National Congress was also a constant thorn in the side of the British. Chirol complains that it "assumed unto itself almost from the beginning the functions of a Parliament. There was and is no room for a Parliament in India, because, so long as British rule remains a reality, the government of India, as Lord Morley [the secretary of state] has plainly stated, must be an autocracy—benevolent and full of sympathy with Indian ideas, but still an autocracy" (p. 154). There were also the difficulties that

10. "There can never be between Englishmen and Indians the same continuity of historical traditions, of racial affinity, of social institutions, of customs and beliefs that exist between people of our own stock throughout the British Empire, the absence of these sentimental bonds, which cannot be artificially forged, makes it impossible that we should ever concede to India the rights of self-government which we have willingly conceded to the great British communities of our own race" (Chirol, *Indian Unrest*, p. 332). Thus the English establishment.

11. J. R. Ackerley, *Hindu Holiday*, rev. ed. (London: Chatto & Windus, 1952). Ackerley went out to India to serve, like Forster, as a private secretary to a native prince. His employer, the Maharajah of Chhatarpur was known to Forster and appears in *The Hill of Devi*. Ackerley's book is of considerable interest because of its similarity in point of view and material with Forster's work and because Forster had read and commented on it.

arise when the civil servants in the field, those Englishmen having direct dealings with Hindus and Moslems in India, are being directed by an administration in White- hall whose knowledge of matters Indian might be in- considerable, but whose familiarity with the domestic political situation was acute. Chirol is consistently in favor of a more active role in the government of India for the viceroy and his council.

Education was a particularly troubling problem for the rulers. English having replaced Persian during the previous century as the official language of learning, large numbers of Englishmen had to be found to staff the schools. Chirol feels that the recommendations of the Public Service Commission of 1886–87, many of which were accepted, intensified the difficulties. He points out that "before the Commission sat, Indians and Europeans used to work side by side in the superior graded service of the [Education] Department, and until quite recently they had drawn the same pay. The Commission abolished this equality and comradeship and put the Europeans and the Indians into separate pens" (p. 213). This information serves as an interesting background for the professional relationship between Fielding and Godbole in *A Passage to India*. Even more relevant is the section detailing Chirol's attitude toward Englishmen teaching in India. Certainly, Fielding is not typical and he is clearly the sort that Chirol—like the English of *A Passage to India*—disapproved of, but it is useful to see the character Forster created set against this idea of the norm for the time and place:

> If it has become more difficult to attract to [the Educa-
> tional Service] the right type of Indians, it has either
> become almost as difficult to attract the right type of
> Europeans, or the influence they are able to exercise has
> materially diminished. In the first place, their numbers
> are quite inadequate. Out of about 500 Europeans

actually engaged in educational work in India less than
half are in the service of the State. Many of them are
admittedly very capable men, and not a few possess high
University credentials. But so long as the Indian
Educational Service is regarded and treated as an inferior branch of the public service, we cannot expect its
general tone to be what it should be in view of the
supreme importance of the functions it has to discharge.
One is often told that the conditions are at least as
attractive as those offered by an educational career at
home. Even if that be so, it would not affect my contention
that, considering how immeasurably more difficult is the
task of training the youth of an entirely alien race
according to Western standards, and how vital that task
is for the future of British rule in India, the conditions
should be such as to attract, not average men, but the
very best men that we can produce. As it is, the Education Department cannot be said to attract the best men,
for these go into the Civil Service, and only those, as a
rule, enter the Educational Service who either, having
made up their minds early to seek a career in India, have
failed to pass the Civil Service examinations, or, having
originally intended to take up the teaching profession in
England, are subsequently induced to come out to India
by disappointments at home or by the often illusory hope
of bettering their material prospects. . . . In some cases
indifference is the worst result, but in others—happily
rare—they themselves, I am assured, *catch the surrounding
contagion of discontent, and their influence tends rather to promote
than to counteract the estrangement of the rising generation
committed to their charge.* . . . The fact, however, remains
that nowadays the Europeans who have the greatest
influence over their Indian pupils are chiefly to be found
amongst the missionaries with whom teaching is not so
much a profession as a vocation. [pp. 227–28. Italics mine]

Forster also considered the influence of the missionaries:
"For the most part they are Christians of integrity, and

fine fellows, too, who try not merely to alter the heathen, but to understand him. It is the missionary rather than the government official who is in touch with native opinion. The official need only learn how people can be governed. The missionary, since he wants to alter them, must learn what they are." [12]

Despite his criticism of clergymen who use their good works in order to make converts, Forster favors the missionary in India over the official. Although the two Anglicans in *A Passage to India* are viewed ironically, serving as the vehicle of Forster's comment on religious confusion, they are treated more gently than the English officials up at the club, a type who "are in India not to live but to rule, and in consequence their experiences are curtailed and their powers of observation atrophied." [13] They "never chew betel—it would not be pukka—and to tell them that one has chewed it oneself requires moral courage." [14] The chewing of betel nut seems to have symbolized for some Englishmen a desire to participate in the ritual—at once trivial and intimate—of Indian life. Ackerley, when he first chews betel, announces only half-mockingly that he is "becoming an Indian." [15] Needless to say, in one of Forster's early letters home from India, he writes that he has become acquainted with betel nut. [16]

12. E. M. F[orster], "Missionaries," review of four books: *In Unknown China* by S. Pollard, *The Rebuke of Islam* by W. H. T. Gairdner, *Women Workers of the Orient* by M. E. Burton, and *Character Building in Kashmir* by C. E. Tyndale-Biscoe, *Athenaeum*, October 22, 1920, p. 545.

13. E. M. F[orster], "Luso-India," review of *The Book of Duarte Barbosa*, Vol. *1*, and *History of the Portuguese in Bengal* by J. J. A. Campos, *Athenaeum* August 27, 1920, p. 268.

14. Ibid., p. 268. Among the connotations of *pukka*, which originally referred to cooked Hindu food, are "authentic" and "superior"—thus, "orthodox."

15. Ackerley, *Hindu Holiday*, p. 140.

16. Forster, *The Hill of Devi*, p. 36. Forster has a full discussion of the subject in "Pan," *Abinger Harvest*, pp. 300–306. This essay first appeared in 1923.

Forster could not have been much surprised by the bigotry, chauvinism, and pompousness of the Englishmen he met in India during his visits of 1912 and 1921, for he must have heard about them at home and occasionally heard them in person, but Anglo-Indians seen in the exercise of their power reinforced his apprehensions and in *A Passage to India* he bared them to the scrutiny of an unsympathetic world. Already in his journal entries during the trip out, he notes the remarks of two English-women: the first declares, "If our children stop in India they get to talk chi-chi and it is such a stigma—we are disgraced"; the second insists, "[The Indians] won't let us know their wives, why should we know them. If we're pleasant to them, they only despise us." [17] The ambivalence of the last speaker is typical. Forster makes no comment upon it. The English were both resentful that the Indians, in separating their women, were thus following a system of exclusion with regard to the English, and contemptuous of the uncivilized views this custom represented. Chirol offers a fuller statement of this curious dualism:

> The bedrock difficulty is that Indian customs prevent any kind of intimacy between English and Indian families. . . . except in the very few cases of Indian families that are altogether Westernized, Indian habits rigidly exclude Englishmen from admission into the homes of Indian gentlemen, whether Hindu or Mahom-edan. . . . On the other hand, it is not surprising that Englishmen, knowing the views that many Indian men entertain with regard to the position of women, do not care to encourage them to visit their own houses on a footing of intimacy that would necessarily bring them into more or less familiar contact with their English wives and sisters and daughters.

A Passage to India contains a dialogue which indicates that

17. Forster, "Indian Entries," p. 21.

Forster's own experience with purdah was somewhat less rigorous. Aziz, who is not an "altogether Westernized" Indian, shows Fielding a photograph of his dead wife. Fielding appreciates this sign of friendship on the part of the Moslem, who then replies:

> "You would have seen her, so why should you not see her photograph?"
> "You would have allowed me to see her?"
> "Why not? I believe in the purdah, but I should have told her you were my brother, and she would have seen you. Hamidullah saw her, and several others."
> "Did she think they were your brothers?"
> "Of course not, but the word exists and is convenient. All men are my brothers, and as soon as one behaves as such he may see my wife." [p. 116][18]

The disagreement about the extent of purdah is part of a large blunder which Forster finds the establishment making: its refusal to acknowledge and act in accordance with the continual changes in the Indian social fabric, its adherence to ossified views that may have been inaccurate to start with. The club in Forster's Chandrapore "moved slowly; it still declared that few Mohammedans and no Hindus would eat at an Englishman's table, and that all Indian ladies were in impenetrable purdah. Individually it knew better; as a club it declined to change" (p. 65). The English also "exaggerate the differences between the various races of India,"[19] differences which Forster admits exist, but not, at that time, to the impossibility of amelioration.[20] Forster is also more sensitive to an English

18. Forster met the Maharajah of Dewas's wife, the rani, after he had been at court only a few days, and the maharajah's mother, the dowager maharani, during his second visit (*The Hill of Devi*, pp. 36–37, 128–29).

19. E. M. Forster, Notes on Egypt, in *The Government of Egypt* (London: Labour Research Department, 1920), p. 10.

20. Ackerley records the Dewan prime minister as saying, "Only fools care about caste." The Dewan, however, had a most independent mind and cannot be considered typical (*Hindu Holiday*, p. 190).

class snobbery which his compatriots take so much for granted as not to notice. Consider Chirol: "The social relations between the two races in India itself—always a problem of infinite difficulty—have certainly not been improved by the large influx of a lower class of Europeans which the development of railways and telegraphs and other industries requiring technical knowledge have brought in their train" (p. 3). Compare with this Forster's treatment of a minor character in the novel: "The wife of a small railway official, she was generally snubbed" (p. 181). Of course, the prejudices of an alien group always appear an absurdity, one's own a reflection of fact. When Chirol tackles the touchy subject of Indian exclusion from Anglo-Indian clubs, he writes: "though a little more elasticity as to the entertainment of Indian 'guests' might reasonably be conceded to Indian susceptibilities, a club is after all just as much as his house an Englishman's castle, and it is only in India that anyone would venture to suggest that a club should not settle its rules of member-ship as it thinks fit" (p. 290). The language of racism has been remarkably static.[21]

Forster, himself, had come to India with a bias. He was opposed to British imperialism, he had made several good friends among the Indian students at Cambridge,[22] he was a long-time foe of all Colonel Blimps.[23] He is one of a

21. See also the response of the collector, Turton, in *A Passage to India*, when he learns of Adela Quested's alleged rape by Aziz in a Marabar Cave: "'that she—an English girl fresh from England—that I should have lived—' Involved in his own emotions, he broke down" (p. 165).

22. "Masood (afterwards Sir Syed Ross Masood) was my greatest Indian friend. I had known him since he was an undergraduate at Oxford, and had stayed with him during my first Indian visit" (Forster, *The Hill of Devi*, p. 100).

23. See, for example, a story by Forster set in Greece and originally published in 1904. "'Drop it, you brigand!' shouted Graham [to a young man who was following someone else's orders by picking up the reins of a mule], who always declared foreigners could understand English if they chose. He was right, for the man obeyed" ("The Road from Colonus," in *Collected Tales*, p. 136).

relatively small group of Britishers which includes his traveling companion, G. L. Dickinson, as well as Ackerley, who published books before the Second World War that ran contrary to prevailing British opinion. In a shipboard conversation with a Frenchman, Dickinson says of Forster, "He, like myself, is a pariah. Have you not observed? [The others aboard ship] are quite polite. They have even a kind of respect—such as our public school boys have—for anyone who is queer, if only he is queer enough. But we don't 'belong,' and they know it. We are outside the system. At bottom we are dangerous, like foreigners. And they don't quite approve of our being let loose in India." [24]

Despite Forster's disapprobation of official British policy and British officials, and his sympathy towards Indians, he could not be termed an Indiophile; his skeptical mind harbored many reservations. When asked by a Moslem to name the greatest defect of Indians, he suggested "the inability to co-operate," which turned out to be an acceptable response. "I might have said untruthfulness or vanity, but they are not accusations that can be borne or profited by. Poor Indians 'll do nothing yet: no constructive policy except vague 'education': but it is character not knowledge they need, and they will get this best by building up a framework of social intercourse. . . . On the other hand a capacity for friendship triumphing over suspicion and forgetfulness [sic]." [25] For the most part, Forster seems more eager to understand the Indian than to criticize him: "The Westerner is on his trial when the Oriental whom he has trusted lies to him. 'A lie is the limit,' he may think, and if he thinks it is, it

24. G. Lowes Dickinson, *Appearances* (Garden City, N.Y.: Doubleday, Page & Co., 1914), p. 5.

25. Forster, "Indian Entries," p. 26. In his notes on Egypt, Forster wrote, "The mild and cheerful Egyptians seemed (especially to one who had known Indians) an easy people to live with" (p. 5). But his second trip softened his attitude.

is, and he had better turn back as soon as he sees the statue of M. de Lesseps at Port Said. Only he can go on who believes that there are different kinds of lies, and that those that are told in order to please a friend must be pardoned, however disastrous their consequences, and though their number be seventy times seven." [26]

The first stop in Forster's 1912 itinerary was the tiny, beautiful Central Indian State of Chhatarpur—"the only idyllic place I have seen yet" [27]—which was to serve as Mau, the setting for the last section of *A Passage to India*.[28] Here he met his first Hindu maharajah and witnessed his first Krishna rites, both matters to be discussed later in this chapter. It was here that he also records in his journal, "Though not more attracted to Indians than I was, I'm irritated by my countrymen more." [29] Chhatarpur was still playing host to "fools" almost two decades later when Ackerley found the brutal dinner conversation of the Anglo-Indians "so remarkable that I began to write it down on the backs of envelopes under cover of the table." [30] It was at Chhatarpur that an Englishwoman asked Ackerley how he liked the people and, when he responded with praise for the Indians, told him, aghast,

26. Forster, "Salute to the Orient," in *Abinger Harvest*, p. 250. This essay first appeared in 1923. Forster's remarks about the Indian character seem particularly relevant to his conception of Dr. Aziz.

27. Forster, "Indian Entries," p. 22.

28. In his notes to the Everyman edition of *A Passage to India*, Forster writes that the scenery and architecture of Mau are derived from two small Central Indian States, Chhatarpur and Dewas (p. xxxiii). It would seem from Forster's descriptions that the interior of the novel's palace is that of the Old Palace in the heart of Dewas (described by Forster in *The Hill of Devi*, p. 161), while the landscape of Mau is that of wooded Chhatarpur at which there was even a temple to Hanuman, a monkey god, such as the one Aziz and Fielding pass on their final ride together. Thus, Forster combined the most beautiful aspects of both areas in his climax.

29. Forster, "Indian Entries," p. 24.

30. Ackerley, *Hindu Holiday*, p. 12.

that she meant the Anglo-Indians, not the natives. In *A Passage to India*, a similar scene occurs between Ronny Heaslop and Mrs. Moore when Ronny cannot figure out the identity of the "nice doctor" his mother has met until he learns the man is not allowed at the club. "Thereupon the truth struck him, and he cried, 'Oh, good gracious! Not a Mohammedan? Why ever didn't you tell me you'd been talking to a native? I was going all wrong.' ... Why hadn't she indicated by the tone of her voice that she was talking about an Indian?" (p. 31). But Mrs. Moore doesn't understand the rules of the game. At the Bridge Party, she says to an intermediary, "Please tell these ladies that I wish we could speak their language, but we have only just come to *their* country" (p. 42. Italics mine).

Mrs. Moore and Adela are exceptions. Forster, Dickinson, and Ackerley found the Englishwoman even more objectionable than her husband. Ackerley writes of the Anglo-Indians, "I felt I didn't like any of them very much—though the men seemed kinder and were certainly quieter than the women."[31] Dickinson says, in a letter home to a friend, "It's the women more than the men that are at fault. There they are, without their children, with no duties, no charities, with empty minds and hearts, trying to fill them by playing tennis and despising the natives."[32] Forster creates a shipboard Englishwoman who exemplifies this type in a published fragment of an unwritten novel. A charming little Indian boy, whom she calls "silly, idle, useless, unmanly," is allowed to play with her children, "but it doesn't matter on a voyage home. I would never allow it going to India."[33] In the vast haze of India, Forster felt that a particular virulence usually

31. Ibid., p. 10.
32. Forster, *Dickinson*, p. 141.
33. E. M. Forster, "Entrance to an Unwritten Novel," *Listener* XL (December 23, 1948), 975.

assails a certain type of Britisher. While serving as a Red Cross worker in Egypt during the First World War, he observed, "Some of the officials have served previously in India; such may be useful for their administrative qualities, but they, and still more their women-folk, introduce a racial arrogance from which the regular Anglo-Egyptian officials are free."[34] It would seem that, for Forster, India presents an especially keen test of character for most English women; Fielding says, "There is something that doesn't suit them out here" (p. 118). Those who are exceptional, like Mrs. Moore, can serve as principals in the kind of novel Forster has in mind, one in which the struggle to achieve, rather than success itself, is interesting and commendable. Those who are typical, like Mesdames Callendar, Lesley, and McBryde, can serve as background. And those who are archetypal, like the collector's wife, Mrs. Turton, can play the Queen of Hearts at Aziz's tragicomic trial: "'He shall not [withdraw the charge against Aziz],' shouted Mrs. Turton against the gathering tumult. 'Call the other witnesses; we're none of us safe'—Ronny tried to check her, and she gave him an irritable blow, then screamed insults at Adela" (p. 230).

After leaving Chhatarpur, Forster went on to the tiny Native State of Dewas, where he spent a week; nine years later he was to return for a longer visit. In 1910, the Indian Native States occupied one-third of the total area of India and contained sixty-eight million people. According to Chirol in *Indian Unrest*, they varied

> in size and importance from powerful principalities like the Nizam's State of Hyderabad, with an area of 82,000 miles—nearly equal to that of England and Wales and Scotland—and a population of over 11 millions, down

34. Forster, *Notes on Egypt*, p. 4n. Ackerley speaks of "the conscious racial superiority which Anglo Indians exhale" (*Hindu Holiday*, p. 104).

to diminutive chiefships, smaller than the holdings of a
great English landlord. Distributed throughout the whole
length and breadth of the peninsula, they display the
same extraordinary variety of races and creeds and
castes and languages and customs and traditions as the
provinces under the immediate governance of the Viceroy, and their rulers themselves represent almost every
phase and aspect of Indian history. [p. 186]

The relationship between the Native States and the con-
trolling power existed rather differently in theory and in
fact. Chirol presents government policy with a coating of
euphemism which makes it sound like laissez faire.

Again, though the relationship of the Supreme Government to all these rulers is one of suzerainty, it is governed
in each particular case by special and different treaties
which vary the extent and nature of the control exercised
over them. In some of its aspects, the principles of our
policy towards them were admirably set forth in a
speech delivered in November, 1909, by Lord Minto at
Udaipur. "In guaranteeing their internal independence
and in undertaking their protection against external
aggression, it naturally follows that the Imperial
Government has assumed a certain degree of respon-
sibility for the general soundness of their administration,
and would not consent to incur the reproach of being an
indirect instrument of misrule. There are also certain
matters in which it is necessary for the Government of
of India to safeguard the interests of the community as a
whole, as well as those of the Paramount Power, such as
railways, telegraphs, and other services of an Imperial
Character." At the same time the Viceroy wisely laid
great stress on the fact that, in pursuance of the pledges
given by the British Crown to the rulers of the Native
States, "our policy is with rare exceptions one of non-
interference in their internal affairs," and he pointed
out that, as owing to the varying conditions of different
States "any attempt to complete uniformity and

subservience to precedent" must be dangerous, he had
endeavoured "to deal with questions as they arose with
reference to existing treaties, the merits of each case, local
conditions, antecedent circumstances, and the particular
stage of development, feudal and constitutional, of
individual principalities." It is obviously impossible to
enforce a more rigid control over the feudatory States at
the same time as we are delegating larger powers to the
natives of India under direct British administration. [p.
188]

Forster describes a system of human meddling which only
altered postwar conditions diminished. He writes, "The
Political Agent, the British official with whom small
rulers most frequently collide, was formerly an imposing
figure. News of his coming stirred the State to its depths.
He represented the Agent to the Governor-General who
represents the Viceroy who represents the Emperor. Girt
with vicarious authority, he laid down the law on every
conceivable subject, including deportment, and freely
criticized everything and everyone who did not minister
to his comfort. Meanwhile his servants blackmailed the
court officials."[35]

The reasons for the change in government policy after
the war are twofold, Forster says: "The Native Princes have

35. Forster, "The Mind of the Indian Native State," in *Abinger Harvest*
pp. 313–14. The essay first appeared in 1922. In *The Hill of Devi*, Forster, as
His Highness's private secretary, is able, in 1921, to thwart the political
agent's desire to be housed in the palace during his visit; he must accept
accommodations in the guest house. But "a cow has to be milked in person
before the person of Political Agent Adams, otherwise he will feel uneasy
about his tea" (p. 109). In *A Passage to India* the same situation is discussed:
"A few years ago, the Rajah would have taken the hint, for the Political
Agent then had been a formidable figure, descending with all the thunders
of Empire when it was most inconvenient, turning the polity inside out,
requiring motor-cars and tiger-hunts, trees cut down that impeded the view
from the Guest House, cows milked in his presence, and generally arrogating
the control of internal affairs. But there had been a change of policy in
high quarters" (p. 294).

shared in the increased consideration accorded to Indians generally, and they are also encouraged because of their usefulness as counter-weights against the new Nationalism." The Princes, "whose mentality is anything but modern, and whose views of the present are always coloured by visions of the past,"[36] constitute "one of the most loyal and conservative forces in the Indian Empire." [37] Indeed, Chirol thought, although they could hardly be too loyal, they were, perhaps, too conservative. The patriarchal rule in the Native States was further from the aspirations of the Indian National Congress, he believed, than the methods of his own government in British India (pp. 329, 330). At Dewas, Forster wrote, "politically— though not socially—we are still living in the fourteenth century."[38] Yet Dewas was to be Forster's major Indian experience. Of course, he traveled widely through the subcontinent, especially during his first trip. And even in 1921 he spent a month in Hyderabad with Masood and a second month on a trip north. But there is no evidence that his acquaintances included any committed followers of Gandhi, to say nothing of any of the militants who were engaged in terrorist activities at the time. Primarily he knew Moslem professional men and Hindu aristocrats: in *A Passage to India*, his Hindus are quiescent; his Moslems, though more agitated, have no plans. Forster was aware of the limitations of his political contacts. During his second trip, he wrote home, "I don't see, nor am I likely to see, anything of present movements in India, except indirectly; I mean that the Government, frightened of Bolshevism and Gandhi, is polite to the princes, and the princes, equally frightened, do all that they can to stop the spread of new ideas. There are said to be new ideas,

36. Forster, "The Mind of the Indian Native State," p. 314.
37. Chirol, *Indian Unrest*, p. 329.
38. Forster, *The Hill of Devi*, p. 113.

even in Dewas, but they are not perceptible to a Western eye." In another letter, he says of Dewas, "There is no anti-English feeling. It is Gandhi whom they dread and hate." And finally, near the end of 1921, "I have been with pro-Government and pro-English Indians all this time, so cannot realize the feeling of the other party." [39]

Actually, Forster was less progovernment than his host, the maharajah, about whom Chirol writes:

> According to the Rajah of Dewas, one of the most enlightened of the younger Hindu chiefs, "it is a well known fact that the endeavours of the seditious party are directed not only against the Paramount Power, but against all constituted forms of government in India, through an absolutely misunderstood sense of 'patriotism,' and through an attachment to the popular ideas of 'government by the people,' when every level-headed Indian must admit that India generally has not in any way shown its fitness for a popular government." He goes so far even as to state his personal conviction that history and all "sound-minded" people agree that India cannot really attain to the standard of popular government as understood by the West. [pp. 192–93]

It was neither his political convictions nor his questionable abilities as an administrator that accounted for Forster's deep affection for His Highness, but rather his personal charm and the depth of his religious commitments. Forster's relationship with his Hindu friend seeped into his ideas about India and eventually helped set the deepest stratum of *A Passage to India*. When the maharajah died in 1937 Forster sent the following obituary to the *Times*:

> As a friend of exactly 25 year's standing, may I be allowed to add a tribute of affection to the account published in your columns of the late Maharajah of

39. Ibid., pp. 113, 137, 237.

Dewas (Senior Branch)? Whatever his weaknesses as a ruler, he possessed incomparable qualities as an individual: he was witty, gay, charming, hospitable, imaginative, and devoted, and he had above all a living sense of religion which enabled him to transcend the barriers of his creed and to make contacts with all forms of belief and disbelief. I am not the only English person who will mourn "Bahu Sahib," as we called him, and who will never forget his vivid and unique personality, or cease to remember him with love.[40]

Forster's first brief trip to Dewas was most pleasant although nothing seems to have occurred which would foreshadow the close friendship that was to emerge nine years later. The maharajah lent him Indian clothing to wear at a banquet and Forster's comic description of the difficulties presented by his gorgeous raiment suggest Fielding's, when, at Aziz's victory party, he is similarly decked out: "Fielding, who had dressed up in native costume, learnt from his excessive awkwardness in it that all his motions were makeshifts, whereas when the Nawab Bahadur stretched out his hand for food or Nureddin applauded a song, something beautiful had been accomplished which needed no development" (p. 251).

With less good fortune, a political crisis could have marred Forster's visit. Forster first met His Highness as the maharajah was composing a telegram to express his indignation at the attempted assassination on December 23, of the viceroy, Lord Hardinge, at Delhi. Forster's response to the attack is typical of his views on Indian matters: "It is a dreadful business—not only in itself, but because it will strengthen the reactionary party."[41] His fears were well founded. The editorial in the next day's London *Times* begins: "All reputable Indian politicians

40. E. M. Forster, "Sir Tukoji Rao Puar," the *Times* (London), December 28, 1937, p. 14.
41. Forster, *The Hill of Devi*, p. 27.

willingly recognize that they have received very great concessions, for which they are grateful, and with which they are content." Only "anarchists" are dissatisfied, the *Times* reassures its readers. The public must not be "disheartened" by "busybodies in and out of Parliament." The control of India must not be weakened.[42]

A similar expression of Indian disaffection occurred during Forster's second stay at Dewas. The visit of the Prince of Wales (later Edward VIII) called by Forster an "undesired, undesirable tour," occasioned disastrous riots in Bombay which did not serve the intended purpose of discrediting the government, but only provoked reaction in the visitor's favor and placed Gandhi in a difficult position. Forster wrote that the prince "represents no tradition which [the Indians] can recognize—not Alamgir's, nor Sivaji's, nor even Queen Victoria's. He belongs to the chatty, handy type of monarch which the West is producing rather against time. . . . It is a type that can have no future in India."[43] While the *Nation and Athenaeum* published this unpopular view, the *Times* had

42. The *Times* (London), December 24, 1912, p. 5. The Conservative hostility toward Indian sympathizers in Parliament also runs through Chirol's *Indian Unrest* and is noted in *A Passage to India*. Ronny Heaslop says, "I am out here to work, mind, to hold this wretched country by force. I'm not a missionary or a Labour Member or a vague sentimental sympathetic literary man" (p. 50). And again, "[The educated natives] used to cringe, but the younger generation believe in a show of manly independence. They think it will pay better with the itinerant M.P." (p. 33). Collector Turton thinks, "The Government of India itself also watches—and behind it is that caucus of cranks and cravens, the British Parliament" (p. 183).

43. [E. M. Forster], "Reflections in India, 2: The Prince's Progress," *Nation and Athenaeum* (January 28, 1922), p. 645. Of the tour of an earlier Prince of Wales (later George V), in 1910, Chirol had written, "The visit of the Prince of Wales to Calcutta had temporarily exercised restraining influence on the political leaders, and the presence of Royalty in a country where reverence for the Throne is still a powerful tradition seemed to hush even the forces of militant sedition" (*Indian Unrest*, p. 87). Even allowing for the gulf between Chirol's political stance and Forster's, the temper of the time can be seen to have undergone a marked change.

carried a report from a special correspondent whose tone
was entirely different.

> I wish to reinforce what I said yesterday about the
> stupendous quality of the Prince's reception. Today I
> have had an opportunity of hearing the opinion of
> leading Indians of different races who are unanimous in
> declaring that it is a very severe blow to Mr. Gandhi's
> prestige. Every possible appeal has been made to induce
> the people to boycott the Prince's arrival, and not less
> than one-third of the total population of the city was on
> the route. The attendance at the ridiculous bonfire
> proceeding was utterly trivial in comparison.
>
> When the rioting began Mr. Gandhi himself, at one
> of the centres of disturbance, appealed to the crowd to
> refrain from violence, and his appeal was as futile as had
> been the appeal to boycott. Probably in some measure
> the rioting was deliberately provoked by non-cooperative
> leaders in annoyance at the magnificence of the Prince's
> reception, hoping to detract from its effect on the out-
> side world, but, once started, it was simply the rowdyism
> of hooligans who saw their opportunity when the police
> were all occupied on the route of the procession. Much of
> the breaking of glass, stoning of motor-cars, and so
> forth was done by small boys. [November 21, 1921, p. 10]

British policy in India sharpened the disagreement
between Forster and the majority of his class. But his visit
provided him with many possibilities. At Aurangabad, in
the Deccan, it offered him, a short while after he left
Hindu Dewas, the world of Moslem civilization. Forster
has not given his readers as full an account of his journeys
into Islam as *The Hill of Devi* presents of his Hindu experiences. Of a number of short articles he did publish,
none illuminates the study of *A Passage to India* quite so
much as a handful of paragraphs from his 1912–13
journal, printed under the title "Indian Entries," to
which I have already made frequent reference. This

material suggests that if all of Forster's diaries and letters are ever made available, scholars will be able to articulate a complete set of correspondences between the body of *A Passage to India* and the detailed skeleton of events comprising his life in India. Virtually everything will prove not to have been invented, only digested. Consider the connections to be found in all that the diary offers of Moslem India—two and a half pages covering one week Forster spent at Aurangabad with "a friend of Masood's, a young Moslem, by name Saeed," serving as host.[44] One entry reads, "To court with Saeed, but he only signed documents. In the sub-judge's room more went on; civil surgeon giving evidence in murder case. Punkah boy, seated at end of table, had the impassivity of Atropos" (p. 25). This bit serves, of course, as the factual impetus for the famous passage about the punkah wallah in the novel. The informing metaphor has already been created in the journal, that of the distance between man and the forces which determine his fate. For Forster the gulf is shaped ironically by incomprehension rather than by Olympian indifference.

> The Court was crowded and of course very hot, and the first person Adela noticed in it was the humblest of all who were present, a person who had no bearing officially upon the trial: the man who pulled the punkah. Almost naked, and splendidly formed, he sat on a raised platform near the back, in the middle of the central gangway, and he caught her attention as she came in, and he seemed to control the proceedings. He had the strength and beauty that sometimes come to flower in the Indians of low birth. When that strange race nears the dust and is condemned as untouchable, then nature remembers the physical perfection that she accomplished elsewhere, and throws out a god—not many, but one here and there, to prove to society how little its categories impress her.

44. Forster, "Indian Entries," p. 20.

This man would have been notable anywhere: among the thin-hammed, flat-chested mediocrities of Chandrapore he stood out as divine, yet he was of the city, its garbage had nourished him, he would end on its rubbish heaps. Pulling the rope towards him, relaxing it rhythmically, sending swirls of air over others, receiving none himself, he seemed apart from human destinies, a male fate, a winnower of souls. Opposite him, also on a platform, sat the little assistant magistrate, cultivated, self-conscious, and conscientious. The punkah wallah was none of these things: he scarcely knew why the Court was fuller than usual, indeed he did not know that it was fuller than usual, didn't even know he worked a fan, though he thought he pulled a rope. Something in his aloofness impressed the girl from middle-class England, and rebuked the narrowness of her sufferings. [pp. 217–18]

Observed through the eyes of Adela Quested, the punkah wallah enters several of the novel's streams. He is a beautiful man and, like Aziz at the Marabar Caves, a reminder of Adela's physical inadequacy; he is untouchable, an instance of the compartmentalization and social injustice of India; he is godlike, a paradox of nature in a "rational" world and an evocation of a Creator whose presence man seeks. Forster worried that the trial scene contained the greatest number of factual errors in the novel,[45] but surely it is a complete artistic success.

At Aurangabad, Forster stayed at the house which was to serve as the model of Fielding's in the novel. In his journal, he writes, "Saeed drove up as I was having a bath and took me to stop with him in a lovely wooden hall: two rows of triple arches which, like the internal pavilions, were painted blue; my bedroom—half the height—was to right, servants to left. Square tank of green water" (p. 25). Fielding's room in *A Passage to*

45. Forster, Notes to the Everyman edition of *A Passage to India*, p. xxxi.

India is described as very beautiful, "opening into the garden through three high arches of wood" (p. 63). "It was an audience hall built in the eighteenth century for some high official, and though of wood had reminded Fielding of the Loggia de' Lanzi at Florence. Little rooms, now Europeanized, clung to it on either side, but the central hall was unpapered and unglassed, and the air of the garden poured in freely" (p. 70). When he comes to tea, Aziz is entranced by this Moslem setting: "I wish I lived here. . . . See those curves at the bottom of the arches. What delicacy! It is the architecture of Question and Answer. Mrs. Moore, you are in India; I am not joking" (p. 70). That Aziz should discuss the symbolism of Indian architecture at a gathering where Moslem, Hindu, Christian, and atheist are attempting some mutual understanding is not inappropriate. Ackerley writes in *Hindu Holiday* that the Mohammedans build arches—but not the Hindus; they prefer rectangular forms with all the pressure downwards. The Hindus consider the arch with its double pressures both downward and outward as self-destructive: "the arch never sleeps" (p. 184). This contrast between two philosophies of architectural form suggests a way of seeing the contrast between the volatile Moslem Aziz, who has generously given his collar stud to Fielding and whose Western collar is riding up his Indian neck, and the tranquil Hindu Godbole, whose "whole appearance suggested harmony—as if he had reconciled the products of East and West, mental as well as physical, and could never be discomposed" (pp. 72–73).

Forster's smallest experiences in Aurangabad are transformed into the stuff of verisimilitude in *A Passage to India*. Like Mrs. Moore, he is shoeless while visiting a mosque and later fussed over by an edgy Moslem. His host Saeed "would guard and order me and invent imaginary perils of beast and reptile" (pp. 25, 27). In the novel, Aziz says,

"I think you ought not to walk at night alone, Mrs. Moore. There are bad characters about and leopards may come across from the Marabar Hills. Snakes also" (p. 21). It was also during these days with Saeed that Forster first heard the Urdu proverb (p. 26) that he gives to Aziz in the novel: "What does unhappiness matter when we are all unhappy together?" (p. 73). These parallels suggest a strong link between Saeed's character and Forster's conception of Aziz. The novelist has been quoted as saying that "Aziz is modeled on Masood, my greatest Indian friend."[46] But, whereas Forster has written very little about Masood,[47] it is impossible to read him on Saeed without finding Aziz evoked everywhere: "More charm than swagger in the boy," he is "a remnant" of "the vanished Moghul Empire"; "an amiable show off. Energy and sense at the bottom. He is a reckless talker, but realises one has few friends" (pp. 27, 26). Saeed's concluding remark to Forster might well have come from the mouth of Aziz: "The accounts of friends are written in the heart" (p. 27).

Forster's knowledge of the Moslem festival of Mohurram which weaves in and out of *A Passage to India* was derived not at Aurangabad but four hundred miles to the northeast

46. K. Natwar-Singh, ed., *E. M. Forster: A Tribute* (New York: Harcourt, Brace & World, 1964), p. xxi. But Santha Rama Rau writes that "in Saeed, . . . the reader can see the outlines of a sketch for the character of Aziz in the novel" (Introduction to E. M. Forster's "Indian Entries from a Diary," *Harper's* CCXXIV [February 1962], 47).

47. Forster's main eulogy, written in 1937, is a much-quoted passage in the essay "Syed Ross Masood": "My own debt to him is incalculable. He woke me up out of my suburban and academic life, showed me new horizons and a new civilisation and helped me towards the understanding of a continent. Until I met him, India was a vague jumble of rajahs, sahibs, babus, and elephants, and I was not interested in such a jumble: who could be? He made everything real and exciting as soon as he began to talk, and seventeen years later when I wrote *A Passage to India* I dedicated it to him out of gratitude as well as out of love, for it would never have been written without him" (*Two Cheers for Democracy*, p. 292).

at Jubbulpore.[48] Although the tone of one reference to the holiday in the novel is mocking, the Mohurram celebration in *A Passage to India*, which has been totally ignored by the book's explicators, serves a thematic function similar to but not as fully developed as that of the Gokul Ashtami ritual in the last part of the novel. In both cases, Forster uses the realistic description of a religious festival whose observance would naturally unwind into the texture of the Indian scene he is fabricating to figure the main pattern of the section: Aziz's isolation and martyrdom in "Caves," Aziz's reconciliation with Fielding in "Temple." For the rites of Krishna's birth are used as images of unity while the drums of Mohurram sound discordant elegies for a martyred king.

The name *Mohurram* means "forbidden" or "taboo," and hence "sacred."[49] Relying on his original sources, the scholar Ja'Far Sharif writes, "There are various accounts of the history of the martyrdom . . . but all agree in the fact that it was caused at the instigation of Yazīd who, wretched from all eternity, was the ring leader, and it was preordained that he should be the author of [the] martyr-dom. . . . The Persians observe the 20th day of the month Safar in commemoration of the burial of Husain's head at Karbalā."[50] Forster writes, "At the entrance of the bazaars, a tiger made [Fielding's] horse shy—a youth dressed up as a tiger, the body striped brown and yellow, a mask over the face. Mohurram was working up. The city beat a good many drums, but seemed good-tempered. He was invited to inspect a small tazia—a flimsy and frivolous erection, more like a crinoline than the tomb of the grandson of the Prophet, done to death at Kerbela.

48. Forster, Notes to the Everyman edition of *A Passage to India*, p. xxi.
49. Ja'Far Sharif, *Islam in India*, trans. G. A. Herklots, new edition by William Crooke (London: Oxford University Press, 1921), p. 151. The ensuing discussion of Mohurram is drawn from this useful volume.
50. Ibid., pp. 153, 157.

Excited children were pasting coloured paper over its ribs" (p. 192). These various apocryphal details are elucidated in *Islam in India*:

> Besides dressing as tigers, men and boys often join hands and go about singing the Muharram dirges. [p. 159]
> The Muharram, including the tomb visitation (*ziyārat*), may be said to last till the 12th day of the month, but the festival really lasts ten days, known as the "Āshūrā" or tenth. Special buildings are provided in which they set up the standards ('alam), the cenotaphs of the martyrs (*ta 'ziya* [Forster's tazia], *tābūt*), the royal seats . . . , the representations of Burāq, the mule on which the Prophet made his journey . . . to Jerusalem and to Heaven. [p. 157]
> On the tenth day in Hyderābād all the standards and cenotaphs, except those of Qāsim, are carried on men's shoulders, attended by Faqīrs, and they perform the night procession . . . with great pomp, the lower orders doing this in the evening, the higher at midnight. [p. 163]
> In India the cenotaph . . . consists of a framework of bamboo in the shape of a mausoleum, intended to represent that erected in the plain of Karbalā over the remains of Husain. It is usually covered with a network of paper neatly cut, and it is sometimes decorated on the back with plates of mica (*talq*). It is also ornamented with coloured paper formed into various devices and has tinsel fringes, the whole structure being surmounted by a dome which is often contrived so as to move round at the slightest breath of air. . . . Within are set up standards or a couple of small tombs intended to be those of the martyrs. [p. 164]

A disagreement in the novel—the argument about whether the height of the tazias is interfering with the pepul tree branches or vice versa—which seems so specific and idiosyncratic turns out to be a traditional battlefield for Moslem-Hindu differences.

Mohurram was approaching, and as usual the Chandrapore Mohammedans were building paper towers of a
size too large to pass under the branches of a certain
pepul tree. One knew what happened next; the tower
stuck, a Mohammedan climbed up the pepul and cut the
branch off, the Hindus protested, there was a religious
riot, and Heaven knew what, with perhaps the troops
sent for. There had been deputations and conciliation
committees under the auspices of Turton, and all the
normal work of Chandrapore had been hung up. Should
the procession take another route, or should the towers
be shorter? The Mohammedans offered the former, the
Hindus insisted on the latter. The Collector had favoured
the Hindus, until he suspected that they had artificially
bent the tree nearer the ground. They said it sagged
naturally. [Ronny Heaslop's account. p. 96]

In *Islam in India*, we find:

Whenever the Muharram, according to the lunisolar
calendar, chances to coincide with Hindu festivals, such
as the Rāmanavamī or Rāmnaumī, the birth of Rāma,
the Charakhpūjā, or swing festival, or the Dasahrā,
serious riots have occurred as the processions meet in
front of a mosque, or Hindu temple, or where an
attempt is made to cut the branches of a sacred fig-tree
which impedes the passage of the cenotaphs. [p. 167]

Unlike Gokul Ashtami, Mohurram is never given the
center of the stage. But it colors the unrest which serves
as background to the horror of Aziz's incarceration. It is
altogether appropriate that during "the last awful night
of Mohurram, when an attack was expected" (p. 199) the
observances of the Moslem prince's martyrdom should
kindle flames of outrage and compassion for the innocent
prisoner.

Contemplating Hinduism, Forster liked the culture
more than the disorderliness; considering Islam, he liked

the civilization more than the orderliness.[51] "Islam," he
writes in an article in 1922, "is an attitude towards life
which has produced durable and exquisite civilizations."[52]
He thought this phrase so apt he used it again in describing
Aziz in the novel: "Islam, an attitude towards life both
exquisite and durable, where his body and his thoughts
found their home" (p. 19). He is sympathetic especially
as it compares with Christianity.

> Equality before God—so doubtfully proclaimed by
> Christianity—lies at the very root of Islam; and the
> mosque is essentially a courtyard for the Faithful to
> worship in, either in solitude or under due supervision.
> . . . Since the edifice under consideration is a courtyard
> and not a shrine, and since the God whom it indicates
> was never incarnate and left no cradles, coats, handker-
> chiefs or nails on earth to stimulate and complicate
> devotion, it follows that the sentiments felt for his mosque
> by a Moslem will differ from those which a Christian
> feels for his church. The Christian has the vague idea
> that God is inside the church, presumably near the east
> end. The Moslem, when his faith is pure, cherishes no
> such illusion, and, though he behaves in the sacred
> enclosure as tradition and propriety enjoin, attaches no
> sanctity to it beyond what is conferred by the presence of
> the devout.[53]

Forster clearly prefers the mosque to the church. He has
written eloquently of one he visited in Egypt.

> Many years ago, at Cairo, I encountered as a travel-
> ler the ruinous Mosque of Amr. The neighborhood
> was deserted, the sunlight violent. I stood outside the

51. Natwar-Singh, *E. M. Forster*, p. xii.

52. [E. M.] F[orster], "India and the Turk," *Nation and Athenaeum* XXXI
(September 30, 1922), 844.

53. Forster, "The Mosque," in *Abinger Harvest*, pp. 260–61. This essay, a
book review of *Moslem Architecture* by G. T. Rivoira, translated by G. McN.
Rushworth, first appeared in 1920.

enclosure and peeped. There was nothing particular to look at—only old stones—but peace and happiness seemed to flow out and fill me. Islam means peace. Whatever the creed may have done, the name means Peace, and its buildings can give a sense of arrival, which is unattainable in any Christian church. The tombs at Bidar give it, the Gol Gumbaz at Bijapur, the Shalimar Gardens at Lahore, the garden-houses at Aurangabad. But it came strongest from the Mosque of Amr, and I learnt afterwards, with superstitious joy, that others, besides myself, had noticed this; that the Mosque had been in early days the resort of the Companions of the Prophet; that the sanctity of their lives perfumed it; that the perfume had never faded away.[54]

In *The Hill of Devi*, he wrote, "I do like Islam, though I have had to come through Hinduism to discover it" (p. 193). But Forster's mind is ceaselessly questioning, and the peace of Islam proves transient. In the disillusioned aftermath of Aziz's trial, Fielding decides—and Forster probably agrees—"Like himself, those shallow arcades [of the mosque] provided but a limited asylum. 'There is no God but God' doesn't carry us far through the complexities of matter and spirit; it is only a game with words, really, a religious pun, not a religious truth" (p. 276).

It is obvious to any reader of *A Passage to India* that Forster is exceedingly interested in and knowledgeable about Islamic poetry, which is itself usually an expression of Moslem history and religion. In the opening scene of the novel, Aziz, at his ease visiting his friend Hamidullah, begins quoting poetry.

Persian, Urdu, a little Arabic. His memory was good, and for so young a man he had read largely; the themes he preferred were the decay of Islam and the brevity of

54. Forster, "The Last of Abinger," in *Two Cheers for Democracy*, pp. 359–60. This essay, containing notes written earlier, was printed for the first time in *Two Cheers for Democracy*.

Love. They listened delighted, for they took the public view of poetry, not the private which obtains in England. It never bored them to hear words, words; they breathed them with the cool night air, never stopping to analyse; the name of the poet, Hafiz, Hali, Iqbal, was sufficient guarantee. India—a hundred Indias—whispered outside beneath the indifferent moon, but for the time India seemed one and their own, and they regained their departed greatness by hearing its departure lamented, they felt young again because reminded that youth must fly. [p. 15]

The three poets mentioned are different in period or fame:

Shams ud-Din Muhammad, known as Hafiz, was born at Shiraz, the capital of the province of Fars, in Persia, some time after A.D. 1320, and died there in 1389. . . . Upwards of six hundred poems are attributed to Hafiz. Of these the majority are classifiable as Ghazels. The ghazel is a type of short lyrical poem, consisting of from about six to fifteen *baits* or couplets. . . . Almost any poem of Hafiz can . . . be read on at least three levels of significance. . . . In the first place the poems may be taken at their face-value as songs in celebration of love and wine. They express the gay and graceful sensuality of a civilization which had achieved a great degree of refinement and sophistication, and which, in spite of the sternness of the Muslim theology which was its background, allowed a considerable freedom of manners. . . . But at a still further remove is the interpretation in terms of Sufi mystical theology. The images of Hafiz's poetry are to be taken as applicable to the universal experiences of the mystic. The beloved becomes the Divine Lover; separation from Him, in its various degrees, is the Dark Night of the Soul, union with Him the mystic's ecstatic absorption in the Absolute. . . . Thirdly, we must consider Hafiz as a court-poet and panegyrist.[55]

55. Peter Avery and John Heath-Stubbs, translators, *Hafiz of Shiraz* (London: John Murray, 1952), pp. 1, 10, 9, 10.

Hali, who wrote at the end of the nineteenth century, is considered a herald of the Moslem reawakening and a forerunner of his more famous compatriot, Muhammad Iqbal (1873–1931). According to V. G. Kiernan, "Iqbal might be summed up as, in the broadest sense, a *political* poet, one concerned with men as social beings. Art, [the poet] said, has for duty the strengthening of mankind in face of its problems."[56] Iqbal reflects the conflict of India. Should the people look to the land, become nationalists and blur their Hindu-Moslem differences or should they look to their pasts and emerge as two separate peoples? Forster, who is concerned with the here and now as well as keeping a fond eye on the past, writes: "Poets—unless they belong to the school of roses and nightingales ('jul and bulbul')—cannot abstain from this choice."[57] Kiernan agrees: "For a community situated as the Indian Muslims were, it was perilously easy for the real or fancied glories of the past to become substitutes for serious thinking or rational decision."[58]

Thus Aziz's tastes in poetry are eclectic: the medieval mystic Hafiz, the modern thinkers Hali and Iqbal. And a little later, from his sickbed, in a scene whose insights into Moslem psychology and art echo the earlier one, Aziz recites from Ghalib (1797–1869), a great lyricist in Urdu of "roses and nightingales":

> Issuing still farther from his quilt, he recited a poem by Ghalib. It had no connection with anything that had gone before, but it came from his heart and spoke to theirs. They were overwhelmed by its pathos; pathos, they agreed, is the highest quality in art; a poem should

56. V. G. Kiernan, trans., *Poems from Iqbal* (London: John Murray, 1955), p. xviii.

57. E. M. Forster, "The Poetry of Iqbal," review of *The Secrets of Self* by Sheikh Muhammed Iqbal, translated from the Persian by R. A. Nicholson, *Athenaeum*, December 10, 1920, p. 803.

58. Kiernan, *Poems from Iqbal*, p. xvii.

touch the hearer with a sense of his own weakness, and should institute some comparison between mankind and flowers. The squalid bedroom grew quiet; the silly intrigues, the gossip, the shallow discontent were stilled, while words accepted as immortal filled the indifferent air. Not as a call to battle, but as a calm assurance came the feeling that India was one; Moslem; always had been; an assurance that lasted until they looked out of the door. Whatever Ghalib had felt, he had anyhow lived in India, and this consolidated it for them: he had gone with his own tulips and roses, but tulips and roses do not go. . . .

The poem had done no "good" to anyone, but it was a passing reminder, a breath from the divine lips of beauty, a nightingale between two worlds of dust. Less explicit than the call to Krishna, it voiced our loneliness nevertheless, our isolation, our need for the Friend who never comes yet is not entirely disproved. [pp. 105–6]

This important connection between Aziz's appeal to the Friend and Godbole's call to Krishna will be considered more fully in Chapter 5. Here, the word *Friend* needs some discussion. Aziz explains it in a later conversation with Fielding: "The Friend: a Persian expression for God."[59] And it appears in Aziz's thoughts at the end of the novel: "A poem about Mecca—the Caaba of Union—the thornbushes where pilgrims die before they have seen the Friend—they flitted next; he thought of his wife; and then

59. "Let us talk about poetry." [Fielding] turned his mind to the innocuous subject. "You people are sadly circumstanced. Whatever are you to write about? You cannot say, 'The rose is faded,' for evermore. We know it's faded. Yet you can't have patriotic poetry of the 'India, my India' type, when it's nobody's India."

"I like this conversation. It may lead to something interesting."

"You are quite right in thinking that poetry must touch life. When I knew you first, you used it as an incantation."

"I was a child when you knew me first. Everyone was my friend then. The Friend: a Persian expression for God. But I do not want to be a religious poet either" (p. 277).

the whole semi-mystic, semi-sensuous overturn, so char-
acteristic of his spiritual life, came to end like a landslip
and rested in its due place, and he found himself riding in
the jungle with his dear Cyril" (p. 320). This curious
passage needs analysis but has never received any. In his
notes to the Everyman edition of *A Passage to India*,
Forster says that the poem Aziz thinks of is from the
Mesnevi of Jalal-ud-din Rumi, "a work to which there
are other allusions in Aziz's talk" (p. xxxvii). I do not
find the poem in the *Mesnevi*, but rather in Rumi's other
major collection, *Divani Shamsi Tabriz*. It is titled "The
Call of The Beloved."

> Every morning a voice comes to thee from heaven:
> "When thou lay'st the dust of the way, thou win'st
>   thy way to the goal."
> On the road to the Ka'ba of Union, lo, in every
>   thorn-bush
> Are thousands slain of desire who manfully yielded
>   up their lives.
> Thousands sank wounded on this path, to whom
>   there came not
> A breath of the fragrance of Union, a token from
>   the neighborhood of the Friend.

Another version of the poem appears in the *Divani*, titled
"The Road Be Thine Towards The Shrine."

> O honoured guest in Love's high feast, O bird of
>   the angel-sphere,
> 'Tis cause to weep, if thou wilt keep thy habitation
>   here.
> A voice at morn to these is borne—God whispers to
>   the soul—
> "If on the way the dust thou lay, thou soon wilt gain
>   the goal."
> The road be thine toward the Shrine! and lo, in
>   bush and briar,

The many slain of Love and pain in flower of young
  desire,
Who on the track fell wounded back and saw not,
  ere the end,
A ray of bliss, a touch, a kiss, a token of the Friend![60]

On the authority of Forster's statement that Rumi's
poetry is important to Aziz, a closer study of this Persian
mystic is indicated.[61] The essential fact of Rumi's life
(A.D. 1207–73) is that he was a Sufi. According to F.
Hadland Davis, "the word Sufi is derived from *suf*,
meaning 'wool.' When a little Persian sect at the end of the
eighth century A.D. broke away from the orthodox
Muslim religion, and struck out on an independent path,
they ignored costly robes and worldly ostentation and clad
themselves in a white wool garment. Hence they were
known as 'wool wearers,' or Sufis." The Sufis owed a
great deal to the Neoplatonists.

> The Cry for the Beloved was in their hearts before the
> Greek philosophers came; but Neo-Platonism appealed
> to their oriental minds. . . . The Neo-Platonists believed
> in the Supreme Good as the Source of all things.
> Self-existent, it generated from itself. Creation was
> the reflection of its own Being. Nature, therefore, was
> permeated with God. Matter was essentially non-
> existent, a temporary and ever-moving shadow for the
> embodiment of the Divine. The Neo-Platonists believed
> that by ecstasy and contemplation of the All-Good, man
> would rise to that Source from whence he came. These
> points bear directly upon the Sufi teaching.[62]

The Sufis strongly opposed the idea of free will or a distinct

60. F. Hadland Davis, ed., *The Persian Mystics: Jalalu'd-Din Rumi* (London: John Murray, 1907), pp. 60, 63, 64. Both versions of the poem are found in this text.

61. Forster also describes Rumi as Iqbal's own master in "The Poetry of Iqbal," p. 804.

62. Davis, *The Persian Mystics*, pp. 11, 13, 12.

and self-existent personality apart from the Godhead,
the beloved. Their growing pantheism led to the idea that
the beloved and lover were identical. This notion, shared
with Hindu mysticism, is the reverse of orthodox Mohammedanism, which holds, like Christianity, that the nature
of God and the nature of man are different.

Despite Aziz's hostility to Hinduism, he possesses a
strain which answers to Rumi's mysticism. And Rumi's
mysticism is essentially Godbole's. Sufism is "a religion of
Love without a creed or dogma. No merciless hells leap
up in the Sufi's belief. He has no *one way* theory for the
Life beyond: 'The ways of God are as the number of souls
of men'."[63] Thus it is not surprising that when Aziz seeks,
through Persian poetry, the Friend (p. 106), Forster
evokes Godbole's song, calling Krishna to "Come, Come."
Compare this poem of Rumi's:

> Come! Come! Thou art the Soul, the Soul so dear,
>   revolving!
> Come! Come! Thou art the Cedar, the Cedar's
>   Spear, revolving!
> Oh, come! The well of Light up-bubbling springs;
> And Morning Stars exult, in Gladness sheer,
>   revolving![64]

Professor Godbole tells Mrs. Moore that Krishna "neg-
lects to come" (p. 80), and in the poem that flits through
Aziz's mind about the Caaba of Union (literally a sacred
building of Mecca) the pilgrims die before they attain
even "a breath of the fragrance of Union." Aziz associates with this intense longing for completion thoughts
about his dead wife. Earlier in the novel he had mused
about her: "She had gone, there was no one like her, and
what is that uniqueness but love? . . . Would he meet her
beyond the tomb? Is there such a meeting-place? Though

63. Ibid., p. 27.
64. Ibid., p. 36.

orthodox, he did not know" (p. 55). But, instead of being depressed by these ideas, Aziz seems revived by them, as if he had experienced something akin to Mrs. Moore's earlier sensation: "A sudden sense of unity . . . passed into the old woman and out, like water through a tank, leaving a strange freshness behind" (pp. 29–30). How this "sense of unity" can arise for Aziz out of its apparent frustration is hinted at in the phrase Forster uses at this point to describe the movement of his spiritual life—a "semi-mystic, semi-sensuous overturn." Sufism, like most mysticism, embodies the abstract desire for union with the beloved in a *vision* of potential consummation so beautiful that the supplicant is often left temporarily satisfied. So, Aziz's soul, impelled to its limit, comes to rest in the serene awareness that he is out riding with his dear friend Cyril Fielding. In denying the fragrance of union, the poet has evoked it.

All of the experiences from the 1912 trip and all that Forster read and wrote about India in the next eight years were not enough to get his embryonic novel born.[65] For this, although he did not know it at the time, he needed the labor of love he performed as private secretary at Dewas in 1921.[66] In *The Hill of Devi*, Forster writes: "I began the novel before my 1921 visit, and took out the opening chapters with me, with the intention of continuing them. But as soon as they were confronted with the country they purported to describe, they seemed to

65. Forster's knowledge of India was varied and extensive. Between his first trip and the publication of *A Passage to India* he wrote thirty articles about the country, including eighteen reviews dealing with at least twice again as many books on Indian subjects.

66. Englishmen employed in Native States were looked at somewhat askance by the establishment. Ronny Heaslop's attitude in the novel is typical: "He did not approve of English people taking service under the Native States, where they obtained a certain amount of influence, but at the expense of the general prestige" (p. 92).

wilt and go dead and I could do nothing with them. I used
to look at them of an evening in my room at Dewas, and
felt only distaste and despair. The gap between India
remembered and India experienced was too wide. When
I got back to England the gap narrowed, and I was able
to resume" (p. 238). But he gives a more interesting, less
frequently discussed, account elsewhere: "I had a great
deal of difficulty with the novel, and thought I would never
finish it. I began it in 1912, and then came the war. I took
it with me when I returned to India in 1921, but found
what I had written wasn't India at all. It was like sticking
a photograph on a picture. However, I couldn't *write* it
when I was in India. When I got away, I could get on
with it."[67] Despite the modern view that photography is
an art, clearly Forster's simile is intended to denigrate his
early attempts with the book as lifeless—an accurate
representation of the details with the vital understanding
missing. Adela Quested has the same problem in the novel
itself. She observes the façade "But the force that lies
behind colour and movement would escape her. . . . She
would see India always as a frieze, never as a spirit, and
she assumed that it was a spirit of which Mrs. Moore had
had a glimpse" (p. 47).

The 1921 trip was not merely another opportunity for
more sightseeing and more anecdotes, although Forster
again collected much material for the novel.[68] Rather, it
was the person of the maharajah, serving as a catalyst,
which set off Forster's productive ferment. Speaking of the

67. P. N. Furbank and R. J. M. Haskell, "The Art of Fiction," an interview with E. M. Forster, *Paris Review* I (Spring 1953), 33.

68. The snake of *A Passage to India* which turns into a branch which turns
back, perhaps, into a snake (page 140) first appears, as many critics have
remarked, on page 91 of *The Hill of Devi*. The ghost who comes back as an
animal which attacks the Nawab Bahadur's car on page 88 of the novel has
his original on page 134 of *The Hill of Devi* in an autobiographical story told
by His Highness.

response to *The Hill of Devi*, Forster said, "You know, nobody seems to have guessed what the book is about. Yes, my friend [the maharajah] was a sort of saint. Who would understand that?"[69] Through his conversations with His Highness, recorded in *The Hill of Devi*, the novelist began to understand a good deal about the cohesiveness of Hindu cosmogony:

> He believes that we—men, birds, everything—are part of God, and that men have developed more than birds because they have come nearer to realising this.
>
> That isn't so difficult; but when I asked why we had any of us ever been severed from God, he explained it by God becoming unconscious that we were parts of him, owing to his energy at some time being concentrated elsewhere. "So," he said, "a man who is thinking of something else may become unconscious of the existence of his own hand for a time, and feel nothing when it is touched." Salvation, then, is the thrill which we feel when God again becomes conscious of us, and all our life we must train our perceptions so that we may be capable of feeling when the time comes.
>
> I think I see what lies at the back of this—if you believe that the universe was God's conscious creation, you are faced with the fact that he has consciously created suffering and sin, and this the Indian refuses to believe. "We were either put here intentionally or unintentionally," said the Rajah, "and it raises fewer difficulties if we suppose it was unintentionally."
>
> I expect that as I have tried to describe it to you, this reads more like a philosophy than religion, but it is inspired by his belief in a being who, though omnipresent, is personal, and whom he calls Krishna. [pp. 45–46]

This idea that God may train his consciousness in one direction while another area is deprived of divine light

69. Raja Rao, in *E. M. Forster*, ed. K. Natwar-Singh, p. 28.

appears in only a slightly different form in *A Passage to India*. Professor Godbole is discussing the Hindu conception of good and evil with Fielding shortly after Aziz's imprisonment. He says: "All perform a good action, when one is performed, and when an evil action is performed, all perform it. . . . When evil occurs, it expresses the whole universe. Similarly when good occurs. . . . [Good and evil] are not what we think them, they are what they are, and each of us has contributed to both. . . . [They] are different, as their names imply. But, in my own humble opinion, they are both of them aspects of my Lord. He is present in the one, absent in the other, and the difference between presence and absence is great, as great as my feeble mind can grasp. Yet absence implies presence, absence is not non-existence, and we are therefore entitled to repeat, 'Come, come, come, come'" (pp. 177–78). After this explanation, Godbole begins what Fielding sees as an irrelevant digression—the story of the Tank of the Dagger.[70] "It concerned a Hindu Rajah who had slain his own sister's son, and the dagger with which he performed the deed remained clamped to his hand until in the course of years he came to the Marabar Hills, where he was thirsty and wanted to drink but saw a thirsty cow and ordered the water to be offered to her first, which, when done, 'dagger fell from his hand, and to commemorate miracle he built Tank'" (p. 179). Rather than a non sequitur, the tale is actually a parable illustrating the metaphysics Godbole has just propounded. This Hindu Ancient Mariner's act of compassion is the outward sign that he is once more in the presence of God's consciousness.

Another Hindu ruler, the Maharajah of Chhatarpur, whom Forster characterizes as "nonsensical and elusive,"

70. According to his notes for the Everyman edition of the novel, the story of the Tank of the Dagger is a local legend Forster heard in the Barabar Hills vicinity (p. xii).

also discussed Krishna with him: "I try to meditate on Krishna. I do not know that he is a god, but I love Love and Beauty and Wisdom and I find them in his history. I worship and adore him as a man. If he is divine he will notice me for it and reward me, if he is not, I shall become grass and dust like the others." Although he was unlike the Maharajah of Dewas, "their different temperaments converged in the adoration of Krishna, and they have between them helped to illuminate Indian religion for me."[71]

The climax of Forster's stay at Dewas, like the climax of *A Passage to India*, was the celebration of Gokul Ashtami, the eight-day feast in honor of Krishna who was born at Gokul near Muttra. Forster felt fairly intimate with the god; he writes that he "has attended his birth and festival at Dewas; has seen his palace dances at Chhatarpur; has read the Bhagavad Gita and the tenth book of the Bhagavata Purana; possesses a picture by Jamini Roy of a young farmer claiming distant cousinhood; is indeed on nearer nodding terms with Krishna than any other God."[72]

The literary authorities for the Krishna birth stories, Forster writes, are the Bhagavata Purana, book 10, and the Vishnu Purana, book 5.[73] The latter source announces the

71. Forster, *The Hill of Devi*, pp. 47–48.

72. E. M. Forster, "The Blue Boy," review of *The Loves of Krishna* by W. G. Archer, *Listener* LVII (March 14, 1957), 444. Forster's discussion of the Bhagavad-Gita was published in *Abinger Harvest* as "Hymn before Action," pp. 324–26. This essay first appeared in 1912.

73. Forster, *The Hill of Devi*, p. 178. Actually, there is a greater difference between the two Puranas than Forster, who had not read the Vishnu Purana (see Raja Rao, in *E. M. Forster*, ed. K. Natwar-Singh, p. 25), realizes. The famous scene in which Krishna steals the gopis' clothing while they are bathing is missing from the latter, along with many other indecorous incidents. In broad outline, however, the two works are similar. The Puranas are "compendious anthologies, comparable in character to the Bible, containing cosmogonic myths, ancient legends, theological, astronomical, and nature lore." Heinrich Zimmer, *Philosophies of India*, ed. Joseph Campbell (Cleveland: World Publishing Co., 1956), p. 62n.

nativity as follows: "In the night of the eighth lunation of the dark half of the month Nabhas, in the season of the rains, I [Vishnu, incarnated as Krishna] shall be born."[74] Thus, the nativity celebration still occurs during the rainy season at Mau several millennia later. Krishna's survival, like Moses', is due to intervention: when King Kamsa— whom Forster compares to Herod, but who also finds a parallel in the Pharaoh of the first two chapters of Exodus—learns on his sister's wedding day that he will be killed by one of her sons, he decrees that all her future children be destroyed. But Krishna is spirited away to the village of Gokul, where he grows up among the herdsmen. There are many allusions in "Temple" to the Bhagavata Purana as well as to other Krishna lore which can be illuminated.

The last section of the novel opens in the palace at Mau to the chanting of "Tukaram, Tukaram, / Thou art my father and mother and everybody" (p. 283). On the next page, when the incantation is repeated, Forster writes, "They sang not even to the God who confronted them, but to a saint." And the chant continues throughout the chapter. The basis of the rite is found at Dewas; "'Tukaram, Tukaram, thou are my father and my mother and all things' we would sing, time after time, until we seemed to be worshipping a poet."[75] An important aspect of Tukaram was his close friendship with the great Maratha warrior Sivaji. Because the maharajah's family originally came from Maratha in the south, this patriotic element was heightened in the Gokul Ashtami celebration at Dewas. Sivaji, born in 1627, was the founder of Maratha power in India. From an early age he "regarded himself as appointed to free the

74. *The Vishnu Purana*, trans. H. H. Wilson, 6 vols. (London, 1864), IV: 261. Nabhas is the same month as Sravana—July and August.

75. Forster, *The Hill of Devi*, p. 178.

Hindus from the Mahommedan yoke. . . . By dint of playing off his enemies against each other and by means of treachery, assassination and hard fighting, Sivaji won for the Mahrattas practical supremacy in western India." [76]

The features of the celebration in the novel correspond almost perfectly with those described in *The Hill of Devi*. From the latter: "the altar is a mess of little objects, stifled with rose leaves, the walls are hung with deplorable oleographs, the chandeliers, draperies—everything bad. . . . The altar was as usual smothered in mess and the gold and silver and rich silks that make up its equipment were so disposed as to produce no effect. Choked somewhere in rose leaves, lay chief Dolly, but I could not locate him" (pp. 159–60, 164). From the novel: "Where was the God Himself, in whose honour the congregation had gathered? Indistinguishable in the jumble of His own altar, huddled out of sight amid images of inferior descent, smothered under rose-leaves, overhung by oleographs, outblazed by golden tablets representing the

76. *Encyclopaedia Britannica*, 11th ed., s.v. "Sivaji." This is the same Sivaji evoked by Aziz when he entertains momentarily the bizarre notion that it was Fielding, perhaps, who followed Adela into the cave: "Such treachery—if true—would have been the worst in Indian history; nothing so vile, not even the murder of Afzul Khan by Sivaji" (p. 280). The *EB* relates: "In 1659 he lured Afzul Khan, the Bijapur general, into a personal conference, and killed him with his own hand, while his men attacked and routed the Bijapur army." The rest of this entry deserves to be given: "In 1666 he visited the Mogul Emperor, Aurangzab, at Delhi, but on his expressing dissatisfaction at not being treated with sufficient dignity, he was placed under arrest. Having effected his escape in a sweetmeat basket, he raised the standard of revolt, assumed the title of raja, and the prerogative of coining money in his own name. But whilst at the height of his power he died on the 5th of April 1680 at the age of fifty-three. Sivaji was an extraordinary man, showing a genius both for war and for peaceful administration; but he always preferred to obtain his ends by fraud rather than by force. He is the national hero of the Mahrattas, by whom he is regarded almost as a deity."

Rajah's ancestors, and entirely obscured, when the wind blew, by the tattered foliage of a banana" (p. 285).

Despite the flippant tone, even more pronounced in the memoir, Forster is struck by the authenticity of the religious fervor the people are experiencing. He writes in *The Hill of Devi*: "Only one thing is beautiful—the expression on the faces of the people as they bow to the shrine" (p. 160). And in *A Passage to India*: "When the villagers broke cordon for a glimpse of the silver image, a most beautiful and radiant expression came into their faces, a beauty in which there was nothing personal, for it caused them all to resemble one another during the moment of its indwelling, and only when it was withdrawn did they revert to individual clods" (p. 284). Chief among the ecstatic is the Maharajah-Godbole figure. What, asks Forster, did the maharajah feel "when he danced like King David before the altar? . . . He felt as King David and other mystics have felt when they are in the mystic state. . . . He was convinced that he was in touch with the reality he called Krishna. And he was unconscious of the world around him. 'You can come in during my observances tomorrow and see me if you like, but I shall not know that you are there,' he once told Malcolm. And he didn't know" (p. 175). Godbole is in the same state: "He came back to the strip of red carpet and discovered that he was dancing upon it. Up and down, a third of the way to the altar and back again, clashing his cymbals, his little legs twinkling, his companions dancing with him and each other" (p. 286).

Dancing is an important part of the Krishna worship. Forster had first seen such dances at Chhatarpur, though he says there was no tradition behind them: "Krishna and Radha wore black and gold. What to describe—their motions or my emotions? Love in which there neither was nor desired to be sensuality, though it was excited at the crisis and reached ecstasy. From their quieter dancing, dignity and peace. The motions are vulgarised by words— little steps, revolutions, bounds, knee-dancing—how clumsy it gets and will my memory always breathe life into it? Radha was most beautiful and animated, but a little touched by modernity; and Krishna, hieratic, his face unmoved while his body whirled, soared highest."[77] Dickinson and Ackerley also wrote about the dances at Chhatarpur.[78] Krishna, says Ackerley, did an exciting dance that got faster and faster ending with his sinking to the carpet; "he whirled like a top on his knees."[79] And Dickinson writes:

> Suddenly, as though they could resist no longer, the dancers, who had not moved, leapt from the platform and began their dance. It was symbolical; Krishna was its centre, and the rest were wooing him. Desire and its frustration and fulfilment were the theme. Yet it was not sensual, or not merely so. The Hindus interpret in a religious spirit this legendary sport of Krishna with the milkmaids. It symbolises the soul's wooing of God. And so these boys interpreted it. Their passion, though it included the flesh, was not of the flesh. The mood was rapturous, but not abandoned; ecstatic, but not orgiastic. There were moments of a hushed suspense when hardly a muscle moved; only the arms undulated and the feet and hands vibrated. Then a break into swift whirling, on the toes or on the knees, into leaping and stamping, swift flight and pursuit. A pause again; a slow march; a rush with twinkling feet; and always, on those young faces, even in the moment of most excitement, a look of solemn rapture, as though they were carried out of themselves into the divine. I have seen dancing more

77. Forster, "Indian Entries," p. 24.
78. Forster acknowledges this in *The Hill of Devi*, p. 182; "Indian Entries," p. 23; and in the notes to the Everyman edition of *A Passage to India*, p. xxxvi.
79. Ackerley, *Hindu Holiday*, p. 34.

accomplished, more elaborate, more astonishing than this. But never any that seemed to me to fulfil so well the finest purposes of the art. The Russian ballet, in the retrospect, seems trivial by comparison. It was secular; but this was religious. For the first time I seemed to catch a glimpse of what the tragic dance of the Greeks might have been like.[80]

Like the Maharajah of Chhatarpur, the rajah in *A Passage to India*

> owned a consecrated troupe of men and boys, whose duty it was to dance various actions and meditations of his faith before him. Seated at his ease, he could witness the Three Steps by which the Saviour ascended the universe to the discomfiture of Indra, also the death of the dragon, the mountain that turned into an umbrella, and the saddhu who (with comic results) invoked the God before dining. All culminated in the dance of the milk-maidens before Krishna, and in the still greater dance of Krishna before the milkmaidens, when the music and the musicians swirled through the dark blue robes of the actors into their tinsel crowns, and all became one. The Rajah and his guests would then forget that this was a dramatic performance, and would worship the actors (p. 303).

Five different stories connected with Hindu worship are touched upon in this passage.

"The Three Steps by which the Saviour ascended the universe" refers to an avatar—literally "descent" of a god —in this case an incarnation of Vishnu who strode over this universe and in three places planted his step, possibly in the form of the dwarf Vamana. "The death of the dragon" suggests Kaliya, the five-headed serpent whose "mouths vomited fire and smoke"[81] and whom Krishna

80. Dickinson, *Appearances*, p. 19.
81. John Dowson, *A Classical Dictionary of Hindu Mythology and Religion, Geography, History and Literature* (London, 1879), p. 144.

subdued but spared, at least in the seventh chapter of the fifth book of the Vishnu Purana. "The mountain that turned into an umbrella" is Govardhana, which was raised by Krishna, Laputa-fashion, to protect the villagers against the furious storm of the enraged God Indra. "The saddhu who . . . invoked the God before dining" appears in a comic nativity story that Forster saw at Chhatarpur. "Krishna steals the food of the Pundit who has come to congratulate his mother, for each time the Pundit says grace he heard Divinity invoked and had to come. No fear of repetition. No feeling for climax."[82] J. R. Ackerley, who saw the nativity play at Chhatarpur a number of years later, liked it better than Forster and described it more fully: A priest padded with pillows representing a Brahman with a staff and cooking utensil honors a lady by eating in her presence at the birth of her child. When he calls on Vishnu to bless the food, Krishna, the child, touches it. A chase and pseudobeating ensue. The food is thrown away, the Brahman rewashed. This action is twice repeated. Then, to a question, the child responds, "He called upon me and I came. I am the god Vishnu."[83] This is an instance of Krishna's coming when he has been called, but there is some evidence that the play was written by the Maharajah of Chhatarpur, an optimistic Hindu. The most detailed account of this play has been left by G. L. Dickinson in *Appearances*:

> In ages of Faith religion is not only sublime; it is intimate, humorous, domestic; it sits at the hearth and plays in the nursery. So it is in India where the age of Faith has never ceased. What was represented that night was an episode in the story of Krishna. The characters were the infant god, his mother, Jasodha, and an ancient Brahmin who has come from her own

82. Forster, "Indian Entries," p. 24.
83. Ackerley, *Hindu Holiday*, p. 34. Krishna is the eighth incarnation of Vishnu.

country to congratulate her on the birth of a child. He
is a comic character—the sagging belly and the painted
face of the pantomime. He answers Jasodha's inquiries
after friends and relations at home. She offers him food.
He professes to have no appetite, but, on being pressed,
demands portentous measures of rice and flour. While
she collects the material for his meal, he goes to bathe in
the Jumna; the whole ritual of his ablutions is elaborately
travestied, even a crocodile being introduced in the
person of one of the musicians, who rudely pulls him by
the leg as he is rolling in imaginary water. His bathing
finished, he retires and cooks his food. When it is ready
he falls into prayer. But during his abstraction the infant
Krishna crawls up and begins devouring the food.
Returning to himself, the Brahmin, in a rage, runs off
into the darkness of the hall. Jasodha pursues him and
brings him back. And he begins once more to cook his
food. This episode was repeated three times in all its
details, and I confess I found it insufferably tedious. The
third time Jasodha scolds the child and asks him why
he does it. He replies—and here comes the pretty point
of the play—that the Brahmin, in praying to God and
offering him the food, unwittingly is praying to him and
offering to him, and in eating the food he has but
accepted the offering. The mother does not understand,
but the Brahmin does, and prostrates himself before his
Lord." [pp. 20–21]

"The dance of the milk maidens before Krishna" and that
of "Krishna before the milk maidens," the gopis, have
already been described in this chapter (pp. 65, 66).

The observances in "Temple" abound with references
to milkmaidens, butter, and milk because the cow is
sacred to Hindus and Krishna had been a cowherd:[84]

84. Ackerley was told by the Maharajah of Chhatarpur that "all
Hindoos must take the five products of the cow. It is our religion." They are
urine, dung, milk, curd, butter. He said he took them daily in small
quantities (*Hindu Holiday*, p. 153).

It was their duty to play various games to amuse the newly born God, and to simulate his sports with the wanton dairymaids of Brindaban. Butter played a prominent part in these. When the cradle had been removed, the principal nobles of the state gathered together for an innocent frolic. They removed their turbans, and one put a lump of butter on his forehead, and waited for it to slide down his nose into his mouth. Before it could arrive, another stole up behind him, snatched the melting morsel, and swallowed it himself. All laughed exultantly at discovering that the divine sense of humour coincided with their own. [p. 289]

Forster had also witnessed these holy games and describes them in *The Hill of Devi*:

With a long stick in his hand H. H. churned imaginary milk and threshed imaginary wheat and hit (I suppose) imaginary enemies and then each took a pair of little sticks, painted to match the turban, and whacked them together. (You must never forget that cymbals never cease, nor does a harmonium.) Real butter came next and was stuck on the forehead of a noble in a big lump and when he tried to lick it off another noble snatched it from behind. (Very deep meaning in all this, says H. H., though few know it.) I had a little butter too. [p. 166]

Even though Forster did not always find the jokes amusing or the games fun, he appreciated Hinduism's inclusion of mirth in the idea of deity: "One was left, too, aware of a gap in Christianity: the canonical gospels do not record that Christ laughed or played. Can a man be perfect if he never laughs or plays? Krishna's jokes may be vapid, but they bridge a gap" (pp. 181–82). He expands this idea in the novel: "There is fun in heaven. God can play practical jokes upon Himself, draw chairs away from beneath His own posteriors, set His own turbans on fire, and steal His own petticoats when He bathes. By sacrificing good taste, this worship achieved what Christianity has shirked: the inclusion of merriment. All spirit as well as all matter must participate in salvation, and if practical jokes are banned, the circle is incomplete" (p. 289).

The novel's festival terminates in the casting of the model of Gokul on the tank's waters. At the edge of the water a beautiful young woman is "praising God without attributes—thus did she apprehend Him. Others praised Him without attributes, seeing Him in this or that organ of the body or manifestation of the sky" (p. 314). Forster was once shown a picture by a holy man at Benares which perhaps aided his understanding of the Hindu deity who could manifest himself in a bodily organ.

> It showed the human frame, strangely partitioned. God was in the brain, the heart was a folded flower. Yoga unfolded the flower, and then the soul could set out on its quest of God. Two roads lay open to it. It could either proceed directly, by the spinal cord, or indirectly through one of the Hindu deities who were dispersed about the body. When asked which road was the best, the Holy Man replied "That by the spinal cord is quicker, but those who take it see nothing, hear nothing, feel nothing of the world. Whereas those who proceed through some deity can profit by—" he pointed to the river, the temples, the sky, and added, "That is why I worship Siva." But Siva was not the goal.[85]

G. L. Dickinson also left a record of this visit to the "saint" of Benares. He is not sure that he remembers the entire detailed explanation he received of the picture of the symbolic tree, but his account complements Forster's:

> In the beginning was Parabrahma, existing in himself, a white circle at the root of the tree. Whence sprang,

85. E. M. Forster, review of *The Gods of India* by E. O. Martin, *New Weekly* I (May 30, 1914), 338.

following the line of the trunk, the egg of the universe, pregnant with all potentialities. Thence came the energy of Brahma; and of this there were three aspects, the Good, the Evil, and the Neuter, symbolised by three triangles in a circle. Thence the trunk continued, but also thence emerged a branch to the right and one to the left. The branch to the right was Illusion and ended in God; the branch to the left was Ignorance and ended in the Soul. Thus the Soul contemplates Illusion under the form of her gods. Up the line of the trunk came next the Energy of Nature; then Pride; then Egotism and Individuality; whence branched to one side Mind, to the other the senses and the passions. Then followed the elements, fire, air, water, and earth; then the vegetable creation; then corn; and then, at the summit of the tree, the primitive Man and Woman, type of Humanity. The garden below was Eden, until the sun rose; but with light came discord and conflict, symbolised by the river and the beasts. Evil and conflict belong to the nature of the created world; and the purpose of religion is by contemplation to enable the Soul to break its bodies, and the whole creation to return again to Parabrahma, whence it sprung.

Why did it spring? He did not know. For good or for evil? He could not say. What he knew he knew, and what he did not know he did not. "Some say there is no God and no Soul." He smiled. "Let them!" His certainty was complete. "Can the souls of men be reincarnated as animals?" He shrugged his shoulders. "Who can say?" I tried to put in a plea for the life of action, but he was adamant; contemplation and contemplation alone can deliver us. "Our good men," I said, "desire to make the world better, rather than to save their own souls." "Our sages," he replied, "are sorry for the world, but they know they cannot help it." His religion, I urged, denied all sense to the process of history. "There may be process in matter," he replied, "but there is none in God." I protested that I loved individual souls, and did not want them absorbed in Parabrahma. He laughed his good cheery laugh, out of his black beard, but it was clear that he held me to be a child, imprisoned in the Ego.[86]

Although it is generally thought that the Maharajah of Dewas was the model for Professor Godbole,[87] this holy man from Benares casts a good deal of light on the Brahman's thought and personality.

There is much information available for tracing the connections between Forster's experience with Anglo-Indians and their appearance in his novel, his encounter with Moslem culture and its transformation into the world of Aziz, and his understanding of Hinduism and its expression in "Temple," but for one central aspect of *A Passage to India*—the Marabar Caves—the relationship between the data and the work of art is unclear. Critics have tried to forge links, as can be seen in Chapter 4, but their efforts have smacked of ingenuity rather than conviction.

Forster knew the three main cave groups of India: the Ajanta, the Ellora, the Elephanta. Dickinson has discussed the visit Forster and he paid to the Ajanta Caves in *Appearances*. Forster describes the Ellora group, both Hindu and Buddhist, briefly in his journal.[88] He also reminisces in an article written in 1953 about an earlier visit to the Elephanta Caves, which are on an island near Bombay and are dedicated to Siva.[89] But none of these

86. Dickinson, *Appearances*, pp. 23–24.

87. In an interview with K. Natwar-Singh, Forster said that Godbole was modeled "on a friend," but did not discuss the matter further (Natwar-Singh, *E. M. Forster*, p. xii).

88. Dickinson, *Appearances*, pp. 7–10; Forster, "Indian Entries," pp. 26–27.

89. E. M. Forster, "The Art and Architecture of India," *Listener* L (September 10, 1953), 421.

caves are like the Marabar. They all have paintings or sculpture or some other noteworthy feature, while the chief fact of the Marabar is that "nothing, nothing attaches to them" (p. 124).

Nevertheless, the Marabar Caves are based on actual caves. Forster writes in the notes to the Everyman edition that the scenery of the caves is that of the Barabar Hills. The Barabar Caves, however, are Buddhist and their entrances are ornamented (p. xxi). But the interiors are similar, as the following description by Sir John Houlton indicates:

> South of the range the visitor will see the detached hill called Kauwadol, crowned by a huge block of stone. There was formerly another large boulder on the top of this block, and it was so poised that the smallest impulse—even a crow perching on it—would cause it to rock. . . .
>
> On a low ridge of granite in the southern corner of the valley are the famous Barabar caves. The hard granite of the interior of these caves has been given an amazing polish. The large cave called the hut of Karna bears an inscription which shows that it was made in the reign of Asoka, in the third century b.c. The Sudama and Lomasrishi caves were never completed. The sculptured doorway of the latter clearly imitates a wooden structure. The fourth cave on this ridge is to the east in a large block of granite; it consists of two chambers, one of them polished. This cave also bears an Asokan inscription. There are three more caves on a ridge of the hills half a mile farther east, which were excavated in the reign of Asoka's grandson Dasaratha. The reader of E. M. Forster's book *A Passage to India* will recall the incident of which the scene is in one of these caves.[90]

Houlton does not mention an echo. But there is no

90. Houlton, *Bihar*, p. 40. It will be noticed that Houlton speaks of only seven caves, while Forster indicates a much larger number in the novel.

doubting the locale. The novel refers to Buddha, "who must have passed this way down to the Bo Tree of Gya" (p. 124), while Houlton writes, "Six miles south of Gaya is the great temple of Bodh Gaya, one of the holiest places to Buddhists. It was near the sacred Bodhi tree, the descendant of which stands at the base of the temple, that Gautama Buddha attained enlightenment."[91] But for the experiences of Mrs. Moore and Adela Quested within the caves, no one has discovered any parallels: the answer must be found completely within the imaginative core of the novel itself—both the published version and Forster's manuscripts.

91. Ibid., p. 36.

3. The Manuscript of *A Passage to India*

THE WORLD AT LARGE first learned of the existence of the original manuscript of *A Passage to India* in 1959, thirty-five years after the novel's publication, when the MS was exhibited at King's College Library in connection with Forster's eightieth birthday celebration.[1] The following year, Forster decided to sell the MS on behalf of the London Library, which had suffered a severe financial blow from a legal decision affecting its tax status.[2] The drafts were purchased by the University of Texas for a reported $18,200 and are housed in the university library.

The manuscript consists of what I labeled during my perusal in 1962: MS. A, a holograph written in faded green ink containing a fairly complete draft of the novel; MS. B, also in green ink, about a fourth as long as *A*, and apparently consisting of earlier drafts; MS. C, a typescript

---

1. See the account by Mollie Panter-Downes: "Profiles: Kingsman," *New Yorker* XXXV (September 19, 1959), 51–80.

2. A. N. L. Munby, Librarian of King's College, Cambridge, to the author, May 26, 1960.

of about eighteen pages corresponding to a handful of pages in the printed novel; and four sheets of corrections and addenda. Nothing is dated, and, to compound the difficulties of reconstruction, the verso pages of MSS. A and B contain innumerable variant passages.

All of this material was organized in a doctoral dissertation of the following year by R. L. Harrison.[3] Harrison presents the first printed edition of the novel—published by Edward Arnold & Co. in 1924—as a framework for the insertion of the previously written MS. A, whenever that MS differs from the published work. What only exists in MS. A is placed in parentheses just before the appropriate place in the printed edition; what appears only in the printed edition is underlined. What is neither parenthetical nor italicized is common to both the MS and the published work. Next, after each relevant section, Harrison includes and labels the pertinent *B* passages and the verso pages of *A* and *B*. For the most part, these versions seem earlier than *A*, although much of *A* is really that part of *B* that Forster saved from the discard; some of verso *A* and *B* appears to be closer to the novel than *A* and, therefore, probably written later than *A*. Harrison's general plan is to let the reader move "backward through the evolution of the book."[4]

The manuscript material at the University of Texas may not represent all the drafts and memoranda that Forster made for his novel, even though he said about his method of writing, "I have very few notes. The plot is in my mind.

3. R. L. Harrison, "The Manuscript of *A Passage to India*" (Ph.D. diss., University of Texas, 1964). Students of Forster, myself included, are indebted to Harrison for his labors.

4. Harrison, "The Manuscript," p. xi. All page references in this chapter, unless otherwise noted, are to Harrison's dissertation. Despite the thoroughness with which he has done his job, I am in disagreement with Harrison about the placement of a number of MS passages, as well as his general conviction that the MSS "differ remarkably little from the printed edition."

Then I alter as I go on from day to day." The rewriting is done in "blocks." The ages and past history of characters are "all in my head."[5] However, in working out a methodology for dealing with the MSS, I have made certain general assumptions and the first of these is that the material in Texas probably comprises all of the *Passage to India* MSS that are likely to turn up and constitutes a sufficient body of variants to clarify Forster's intentions in the novel's published version. I am thus also assuming that the work's final form represents the author's deliberate judgment of all the possibilities he discarded. Yet the rejected material must be analyzed for any light it can shed on the choices Forster finally made and any ambiguities in the novel which it can resolve. In order to break into this ring of reciprocity and find a central intention, I posit that each variant Forster selected over other contenders equally vivid was determined by his total conception of the novel, the novel being hypothesized in this view not as an ongoing series of alternatives in flux like each specific choice under the author's consideration, but rather as a cohesive world which exists in its creator's mind and which we believe exists because he seems to be testing the appropriateness of each choice within the context of a certain roughly defined original structure.[6] Of course, there are groups of changes which can be viewed as creating a trend toward a modified conception. But I think that only by viewing each of the hundreds of alterations in all the pages within the larger pattern of Forster's final decisions will the nature of the revisions be understood: some of the text's revisions will be

5. Angus Wilson, "A Conversation with E. M. Forster," *Encounter* IX (November 1957), 56. In another interview, Forster said he felt it "improper" to keep a notebook to record observations for his novels (Furbank and Haskell, "The Art of Fiction," p. 35).

6. "Theme, he thought, came before plot" (Furbank and Haskell, "The Art of Fiction," p. 65).

seen as synonymous with the material they replace—mere stylistic polishing for the sake of clarity, or perhaps, for the sake of less clarity; a few revisions contradict the spirit of their antecedents and are genuine recastings of an incident or idea; but most of the changes are in the nature of reshapings—material that was formerly peripheral is maneuvered to the center, while something that was previously highlighted is dimmed. The alterations take no one direction, so no single standard can be used in judging them. The final test must be the meaning which the whole of the novel demands of the parts, even as the determination of each part limits the possibilities available to the other parts.

To study the MSS of *A Passage to India* is to find the novel more comprehensible: problems of plot, theme, method, and characterization are clarified. The elements of the plot which are constant in all versions underline the basic story that Forster wanted to tell: two Englishwomen— one young, one old—go out to India and are shattered by the experience; the young one indirectly causes a quarrel between an Englishman and an Indian which is finally healed. The different versions of this single plot in the drafts and text only emphasize the pattern of movement the author had in mind: attraction, rupture, reunion. The main themes of *A Passage to India* are most clearly examined by studying the pages in the MSS and published work which treat the expedition to the caves and the festival of Gokul Ashtami. Both cave and temple symbolize the undiscriminating oneness of the universe, as MS passages similar to those Forster eventually created for the text reaffirm. The cave presents this vision bleakly: it was Forster's final decision to have the characters who are, for theological or psychological reasons, most unprepared to cope with the vision, Mrs. Moore and Adela Quested, confront this truth during the expedition.

Ironically, their response to the idea that all things are the same leads to a breakup of human relations. The temple, however, represents the idea that unity is benevolent by encompassing Godbole's brotherly love and Aziz's and Fielding's reconciliation, as well as recapitulating motifs sounded previously in the novel, a device which appears only in the published work. As for Forster's method, a comparison of the drafts with the text reveals that his goal is to entertain the reader by means of contrast: personal and ideological conflicts are heightened in the published work; details are more sharply drawn. Finally, various changes in the characters indicate that some of them—Aziz and Mrs. Moore especially—were gradually reshaped as Forster's theme of fissure and connection grew more prominent. These various subjects will be discussed in the order they have been mentioned here.

All the versions of *A Passage to India* share a similar plot structure which is of interest because it shows that, from the outset, Forster wanted his story to take a certain shape: an old woman and a young girl come out to India on a visit, during which they meet a young Moslem doctor, an English schoolmaster, his Hindu assistant, and various members of the Anglo-Indian community. The visitors are anxious to see as much of India as possible and at a tea party attended by all the principals except the girl's unsympathetic fiancé an expedition to some local caves is arranged. The outing proves catastrophic. The young girl believes that the doctor has attempted to rape her in a cave and he is subsequently imprisoned. The old lady suffers a physical and psychological collapse and, attempting to return to England, dies en route. The Hindu remains inscrutable. At the doctor's trial, his accuser retracts her charges but the strains created by the visit to the caves have grown too intense to be alleviated by the trial's just outcome. The girl and her fiancé are estranged and she goes home. The friendship of the doctor and the schoolmaster also fails to survive posttrial tensions, even though the Englishman has supported the Moslem throughout his ordeal. In an epilogue which takes place two years later, the doctor and the schoolmaster meet again, are reconciled, but then part, apparently forever.

Some of the forms which Forster gave this plot deserve to be examined at this point. In verso *B*, the young girl is the old lady's daughter and makes the acquaintance of her future fiancé after arriving in India. In another draft which resembles the finished novel much more closely, the fiancé is the old lady's son and the girl already knows him—in fact, if she likes him as much in India as she has in England, she plans to marry him. But, in this later draft, the young man has the same name as his mother— Moore—and the old lady has a husband at home, while in the novel Mrs. Moore's son, Ronny Heaslop, is the child of her first marriage, and she has had two children by her second husband, who has left her a widow for the second time. These other children, Ralph and Stella, figure, of course, at the end of the novel, where Ralph's similarity to his mother helps keep Mrs. Moore's spirit a force in the action. Another plot variant concerns the first rupture between Ronny and the girl, Adela Quested. In one manuscript version, they decide not to become engaged after the unsuccessful Bridge Party, very early in the book, whereas in the novel the breach, by which Forster obviously wanted to show their uncertainty, takes place a bit later, after the tea party, and is subsequently mended, only to be reopened as a result of the trial. The discord which arises between Dr. Aziz and the schoolmaster, Fielding, as a result of the tragic expedition to the caves also exists in all versions, but the incident differs in each of them as Forster hunts for circumstances which will make credible this break between good friends. In one draft, Aziz berates Fielding for not having resigned as principal of Government College in protest against his arrest, but the Englishman's defense is so sound—he needs the job if he is to stay in the town and help the Indian fight his case—that, had Aziz persisted in his irrational complaints, the reader would have become unsympathetic toward the beleaguered doctor, a response the author did not wish to elicit. Finally, Forster hit on the compensation that Adela is to pay the falsely accused doctor as a fitting subject for the two friends to disagree about. Fielding persuades Aziz to be modest in his demands and, when the doctor later believes—erroneously—that the Englishman has married Miss Quested, he suspects that his friend has counseled generosity in order to acquire Miss Quested's money for himself; the misunderstanding which ensues discredits neither man. The point is that Forster switched these last situations only to make the plot better serve one of his preconceived themes: the Marabar Caves ignite the evil that is potential in the English dominion over India.

The expedition to the caves is essential to the book's courtroom plot and also to its political theme, but the sequence accomplishes even more than this. As several critics have pointed out, all the movement in the novel leads up to and then away from the Marabar. Forster himself said, "When I began *A Passage to India*, I knew something important happened in the Malabar Caves [*sic*], and that it would have a central place in the novel—but I didn't know what it would be. . . . The Malabar Caves represented an area in which concentration can take place. . . . They were to engender an event like an egg."[7]

7. Ibid., p. 31.

Mrs. Moore's reactions to the caves, unlike those of Adela, have but little effect on the plot, yet, for most readers, they are the novel's center of intensity, rivaled only by Godbole's celebration of the birth of Krishna. The caves and their echo serve as an emblem of India: a mystery of such magnitude that Western visitors like Mrs. Moore and Adela Quested may break down when confronted with it. The collapse of both women is the informing fact of *A Passage to India*. The relationship between Fielding and Aziz is altered by it; Godbole's benevolent Hinduism is its antidote.

Nowhere in the MSS are there so many false starts, abandoned possibilities, reworked and relocated passages as in the pages which were to comprise chapters thirteen through sixteen in the published novel—the visit to the caves. Strangely enough, it was not the complex metaphysical import of the caves that troubled Forster: many of the major speeches can be seen in virtually their final form in the earliest drafts. Rather, it was deciding what sorts of character development would best animate his themes and then stage-managing Adela's attack and flight from the caves that taxed the writer most severely.

In the treatments he discarded, Forster recorded the reactions of Fielding, Aziz, and Adela to the caves. Amazingly, Mrs. Moore does not enter any cave in the earliest version. She begs off because of fatigue. (Forster may have been trying to get rid of the old lady so that Aziz and Adela could visit the caves alone, lending plausibility to the alleged rape. In the novel, Mrs. Moore does drop off after her first cave.) Yet her disillusionment —what Forster once called her "negative vision"—occurs even in MS. B, during the train ride from Chandrapore out to the Marabar Hills:

> Mrs. Moore awoke with a definite and alarming feeling all over her body. She was ill. Heart, nerves, or sup-

pressed gout, the doctors had called such a symptom, but she believed it was spiritual, that the soul can stray out of its kingdom and be caught. . . . Mrs. Moore recovered control, the sickishness and bad taste in her mouth were some relics of something she had forgotten, but that had underlined the loneliness of human life. "What I am through old age, others are in their youth, if only they knew it," was the thought that remained throughout the day. Young people chatter and embrace, but cannot communicate. Their loneliness is fixed, their relationship no more than the concourse of stones in a heap. Yet they stand not in magnificent isolation, as their poets in the west proclaim. They are not captains of their souls, because loneliness proceeds from a larger disaster it has its roots outside of humanity. [p. 276][8]

The substance of Mrs. Moore's thought here is necessarily different from the vision Forster grants her in the novel as a result of her tour of the first cave. There, the echo determines her ideas about unaccommodated man in an indifferent universe. But, in this version, riding before dawn in the train's purdah carriage, Mrs. Moore dozes off. As a result of her nap, she becomes aware of certain thoughts that have been skirting the edges of her consciousness since she arrived in India. Chief among these is the idea of the separateness of human beings, a notion which her Christian faith has previously held in check. This feeling of alienation is not the strongest impression that the novel's Mrs. Moore carries away from the cave— there it is the conviction that nothing has value—but the two responses share one idea, although the idea is expressed more explicitly in the MS: the roots of the horror are "outside of humanity." This is the discovery that lies

8. In order to avoid the nuisance to the reader of the insertion of numerous *sics* in quoting from obviously rough drafts, I am spelling out ampersands, regularizing spelling, and omitting *sic* altogether. Where punctuation is missing or unorthodox, or other solecisms occur in the quotations, they are to be assumed as following the MS.

at the heart of Mrs. Moore's subsequent resignation—the motivation for which is somewhat murky in the novel—her refusal to believe, for example, that Aziz's predicament can be helped by human intervention. It is, as will be seen later, the obverse of Godbole's cheerful passivity in the face of a universe which makes no distinctions.

In another passage from the early draft quoted above, the old lady's mysticism expresses itself in the view that ordinary human equipment is inadequate for experiencing the universe:

> Never before had she felt so detached from her fellows, or had thus despised their efforts to communicate. Wrong—the whole thing wrong—the instrument and signals of human gestures and cries are wasteful mistakes, a stony bypath that leads nowhere. Millions of years of talk and carnal embracement, yet man is no nearer to understanding man. . . . There are colours and sounds we cannot perceive. There is also life we cannot perceive. Man is not the measure, he can only focus a tiny spot, he cannot define what is remarkable about the Marabar Caves. [p. 296]

All that is left of this material during the train ride in *A Passage to India* is an idea that Forster had originally jotted down elsewhere in the margin of the MS as an indication that he wanted to insert it in the most telling place: "She felt increasingly (vision or nightmare?) that, though people are important, the relations between them are not, and that in particular too much fuss has been made over marriage; centuries of carnal embracement, yet man is no nearer to understanding man. And to-day she felt this with such force that it seemed itself a relationship, itself a person who was trying to take hold of her hand" (p. 135).

It is not difficult to feel reasonably sure that Forster decided to postpone Mrs. Moore's collapse because nothing had happened during either the preceding days or the journey sufficiently dramatic to motivate it. By putting the old lady into the cave with the crush of alien villagers, the darkness, the suffocating heat, the stench, and the supremely disturbing echo, the writer had found the objective correlative for his character's profound malaise. Now her subsequent behavior would be persuasive. But, surprisingly enough, Forster had already given the cave encounter to Fielding: in the earliest version, some of her responses are attributed to the schoolmaster; thus, the scene had to be greatly modified.

In all versions of the journey to the Marabar, Godbole and Fielding miss the train; the schoolmaster, however, turns up later, when the expedition is almost over, brought by Miss Derek. There are more reworkings of Miss Derek's rescue of Adela than of any other single incident because Forster wanted to get Miss Quested back to Chandrapore in Miss Derek's car without the other principals finding out what had happened to her—and yet Fielding must arrive in Miss Derek's car. Unaware of the rescue, the Englishman talks with Aziz and Mrs. Moore. At this point, MS. B has Fielding deciding to have a quick look at a Marabar Cave before what is left of the party returns to the city. He enters the cave and begins a remarkable monologue:

> "Have you anything to say?" [he asks the cave]. "Boum." "Of man's first disobedience and the sin / Of that forbidden tree . . ." he remarked. Then he recited, in a different tone of voice, the beginning of a poem that he had once admired even more than Paradise Lost because it was adventurous and sane, and sang of the triumphs as well as the fall of man
>
> > Enter these enchanted woods
> > You who dare

A shout, a whistle, a whisper, all were "Boum." loud or
soft but without distinction in quality. He felt helpless and
terrified, as if someone were insulting him, and through
him, humanity. Once more he spoke, and with a tender-
ness he never admitted into his daily voice. He pleaded
for all the unhappiness and misunderstanding in the
world, past, present, and to come, for the misery we must
all undergo, whatever our opinions and positions, and
however much we dodge or bluff. And the words he
chose for the intercession were not altogether appropriate but they came into his mind, they were four lines
of Persian that Aziz had compelled him to learn.

> Alas, without me for thousands of years
> The Rose will blossom and the Spring will
> bloom,
> But those who have secretly understood my
> heart—
> They will approach and visit the grave where I
> lie.

[p. 337][9]

After reciting the Persian poem, Fielding, alone in the
cave, thinks, "Poetry, piety, courage—nothing has
value." Then, in a moment of revulsion, he shouts, "Go
to Hell!" Whether this final outburst expresses the bravado
of a thoroughly shaken man or Fielding's humanism
rising triumphant is conjectural, but it is difficult to
imagine Fielding, the rationalist, succumbing permanently
to the spirit of the Marabar as does Mrs. Moore. The
following excerpt from the novel parallels Fielding's confrontation; the old lady reviews her experience immediately after it has occurred:

9. Readers of the novel will recognize this quatrain as the poem Aziz
plans to have inscribed on his tomb in the mosque he "some day . . . would
build" (p. 19). In his notes to the Everyman edition of *A Passage to India*,
Forster says the quatrain is from the sixteenth-century tomb of Ali Barid at
Bidar (p. ii).

[The echo] had managed to murmur, "Pathos, piety, courage—they exist, but are identical, and so is filth. Everything exists, nothing has value." If one had spoken vileness in that place, or quoted lofty poetry, the comment would have been the same—"ou-boum." If one had spoken with the tongues of angels and pleaded for all the unhappiness and misunderstanding in the world, past, present, and to come, for all the misery men must undergo whatever their opinion and position, and however much they dodge or bluff—it would amount to the same, the serpent would descend and return to the ceiling. . . . But suddenly, at the edge of her mind, Religion appeared, poor little talkative[10] Christianity, and she knew that all its divine words from "Let there be Light" to "It is finished" only amounted to "boum." [pp. 149-50]

Despite the substitution of the King James Bible for Milton and Meredith, in accord with Mrs. Moore's religious temperament, the impact on the reader of both versions is similar. Forster has created in the echo a rather inscrutable yet powerfully evocative symbol to generate the idea that the central force in the universe long ago obliterated all the discriminations that foolish men still invent.

Adela's and Aziz's responses to the caves are also described in the MS. Aziz is jocular. His Mohammedanism, formalistic and everywhere tinged with pathos at the transcience of love, beauty, and God's light, is too simple and closed a system to leave him vulnerable to the category-denying echo.[11] He says to Adela in a MS. B

10. Only in the novel does "talkative" appear before "Christianity," a late addition which many commentators have found most effective.

11. In the novel, Forster writes of the Moslem creed, "'There is no God but God' doesn't carry us far through the complexities of matter and spirit; it is only a game with words, really, a religious pun, not a religious truth" (p. 276). In the MS he had written, not "religious pun," but "childish pun" (p. 610).

version: "Boum! goes the echo, boum. You ask what date, echo says boum. The villagers shout their silliness and it says boum, you whisper and it's boum, boum, again just as loud, nothing but boum, and this is the kind of thing Hindus call interesting, boum, boum, boum, boum." [12] Aziz receives the same message from the caves that Mrs. Moore does, but it leaves him undaunted: his temperament responds to emotional, human interplay, not metaphysical speculation. Forster decided to omit the doctor's comments. Possibly, he felt that if he retained the reactions of Fielding, Aziz, and Adela, while adding those of Mrs. Moore, he would dilute the caves' impact on the two characters who would be deeply affected by them.

The caves make no *direct* claim on Adela: she is too troubled by her personal problems. In MS. B, Forster writes, "She thought not of the myriad crystals extending behind the polish round her into the hills" (p. 312). The echo, however, becomes the medium through which Adela finds an answer to the questions about love which have begun to preoccupy her out on the broiling rock moments before she enters the cave. Because, unlike Mrs. Moore, she ignores the echo on a conscious level—even though its import is relevant to her doubts—Adela is assailed by its significance in a delusion. There is nothing in the MSS which clears up the question, "What happened in the cave?" On the contrary, some of the drafts aggravate the difficulties: the attack is described more vividly, yet the possibility of the guide or some roving Pathan being the culprit [13]—to say nothing of Aziz—is

12. In MS. B, Forster writes "[The caves] have an echo. And they are polished. Professor Godbole had been thinking of one or other of these characteristics, perhaps" (p. 239). And Aziz is probably thinking of Godbole's refusal either to praise or dismiss the caves when he jeers at Hindu interest in them. Aziz's contempt for and ignorance of Hinduism run through the novel.

13. See Fielding's speculations in the novel, p. 242.

diminished. Had Forster wanted to sustain the likelihood that there actually was an attempted rape, he should have created circumstances that would have left open this line of action. But since he has not, I conclude that Adela's breakdown, like Mrs. Moore's, is self-induced, and, also like Mrs. Moore's, is based on a sudden, powerful—but, in Adela's case, subverbal—realization that all discriminations are meaningless.

For critics who complain that Forster's fiction is pallid because he lacks the ability to write scenes of violence or passion, here is the action he created for the assault in MS. B:

> At first she thought that he was taking her hand as before to help her, then she realized and shrieked at the top of her voice. "Boum" started the echo. She struck out and he got hold of her other hand and forced her against the wall, he got both her hands in one of his, and then felt at her breasts. "Mrs. Moore," she yelled. "Ronny—don't let him, save me." The strap of her field glasses tugged suddenly, was drawn across her throat. She understood—it was to be passed once round her neck, she was to be throttled as far as necessary and then . . . Silent, though the echo still raged up and down, she waited and when the breath was on her wrenched her hand free, got hold of the glasses and pushed them into her assailant's mouth. She could not push hard, but it was enough to hurt him. He let go, and then with both hands on her weapon she smashed at him again. She was strong and had a horrible joy in revenge. "Not this time" she cried, and he answered—or the cave did. She gained the entrance of the tunnel. [pp. 316–17]

Forster probably discarded this treatment, not because it was insufficiently graphic, but because it portrayed Adela's delusion *too* vividly. Who, reading it, would not be convinced that there was a real-life assailant, blood on

the field glasses, other clues? But Forster was not interested in developing this aspect of his story; as will be seen
shortly, he has just about precluded the guide—the only
human being on the landscape besides Aziz—as a pros-
pect. And Aziz, of course, is unthinkable as the villain:
Forster makes this clear in every version. I believe that
there is another reason, aside from its slanting, that
caused the scene to be dropped. As he told Angus Wilson,
Forster liked "a good plot,"[14] and had he retained this
version all suspense would be gone. As the situation
stands in the novel, the reader sees, with only vague
forebodings, Aziz come out of a cave, hunt for Miss
Quested, return to Fielding and Mrs. Moore, and learn
that Adela has driven off with Miss Derek. When the
train returns to Chandrapore, there is the shock of Aziz's
arrest, but it is not until the next chapter that Collector
Turton reveals the charge to Fielding. Forster obviously
worked hard to achieve this sleight of hand.

In the novel, Aziz and the guide hear Miss Derek's
motorcar while Adela is absent, either in the cave or
fleeing down the hill. The guide acts normally. In the
version quoted above, the guide sees a motor approaching
before Adela wanders into the cave and tries to tell her
but she doesn't understand him. With Aziz on hand and
Europeans arriving by car, the guide would have to be a
mad man to try to rape Adela—or be overcome by her
beauty. But the one thing Miss Quested is not is desirable.
The MSS stress this even more than the novel.

Dr. Aziz finds Adela supremely unattractive in the
various early drafts of *A Passage to India*. When he first
meets her at Fielding's tea party, MS. A records his
impressions: "He thought Miss Quested the ugliest
English girl he had ever seen. Her planky body and mottled
face seemed an irreparable misfortune at first sight" (p.

14. Wilson, "A Conversation," p. 56.

122). In the novel he is only slightly less critical: "Adela's angular body and the freckles on her face were terrible defects in his eyes, and he wondered how God could have been so unkind to any female form" (p. 68). And when, in MS. B, Aziz is informed at the police station of the charge against him, he is aghast: "That woman with the flat breasts. She supposed he desired them" (p. 352).

Although in the novel Adela notices on the way to the caves "what a handsome little Oriental he was" (p. 152), both the MSS and the final work make it clear that Adela is no more drawn to Aziz physically than he is to her. The novel goes on, "She did not admire him with any personal warmth, for there was nothing of the vagrant in her blood" (p. 153); MS. A is, if anything, more explicit: "[Aziz] did not attract her in any sexual sense. . . . She was not subject to waywardness" (p. 313). Yet some critics, undaunted by a lack of evidence in the novel, have persisted in understanding Adela's delusion that Aziz has attempted to rape her as a projection of her own repressed desires for the Moslem. What Forster does offer in the way of explanation for her delusion is Adela's sense of her own physical inadequacy: "She regretted that neither she nor Ronny had physical charm. It does make a difference in a relationship—beauty, thick hair, a fine skin" (p. 153). (Her list seems more applicable to a woman.) A reading of the earlier drafts reinforces this idea. In *B*, immediately after she sees the footholds in the rock which remind her of the tire prints of the nawab's car and her subsequent reconciliation with Ronny, she muses that "if the ideal lover had come her way, she would have thrown meagre Ronny aside, but he never would come. For Miss Quested had no illusions about her personal attractiveness. Her vanity was intellectual, and she knew that no one admired her; always, from a little girl, she too had been meagre, so she did not expect a perfect mate"

(p. 311). The novel touches on this idea, but Forster decided not to develop it. Yet it does much to explain Miss Quested's behavior. In one version, she enters the cave and meditates that "probably Ronny didn't 'love' her either and perhaps the reason was that neither of them had beautiful bodies—a humiliating reason, but like all things it must be faced. . . . 'Yes we all have our limitations'" (p. 314). Another version includes, after "beautiful bodies": "It didn't matter how ardent their souls were, the coldness of Matter determined" (p. 314). And at that precise juncture, a shadow shows that someone has followed her down the entrance tunnel. This material, revealing how painfully inadequate Adela feels and how much she wishes to be admired, although not in the published novel, seems to illuminate Adela's personality more fully than the notion, often espoused by analysts, that Adela is overcome in the cave with unconscious lust for Aziz. It is Adela's need to be herself desirable rather than her desire for Aziz that motivates her behavior.[15]

But it is only when she sets the echo uncoiling—by addressing the shadow whom she takes to be Aziz in the MS, by scratching her fingernail against the wall in the novel—that Adela's need triumphs over the common-sensical restrictions of her rational mind and turns into fantasy. The echo is crucial: it affects her, as I have suggested, just as it did Mrs. Moore. Everything becomes equal, not only "pathos, piety, courage . . . and . . . filth," but also beauty and ugliness, one man and another, reality and illusion. Later on in the novel, Mrs. Moore says, "And all this rubbish about love, love in a church, love in a cave, as if there is the least difference" (p. 202). Adela understands Mrs. Moore to have somehow said by

15. The Adela of Forster's MS. B also shows a tremendous amount of hostility in the rape scene (see p. 94), but this facet of her personality is nowhere expanded in either the novel or the other revisions.

these words that Aziz is innocent—although Ronny is certain that his mother has never mentioned the doctor's name, as indeed she hasn't. But Mrs. Moore's remarks temporarily lessen the echo Adela has continued to hear since her experience in the caves. I think this abatement occurs because Mrs. Moore gives Adela an inkling of what the old lady has been able to hear of the echo's meaning; Adela—hitherto unable to face the thought that courage and filth, truth and fantasy, love in a cave and love in a church, are all one—has managed to keep up the echo's roar as a barrier between her and the realization she cannot quite admit. At the trial, when she suddenly knows that Dr. Aziz never actually entered the cave, her echo disappears.

In sharp contrast to the four chapters in "Caves" which deal with the Marabar directly and are, as I have indicated, extensively revised, the five chapters which make up the concluding section, "Temple," are not, with one exception, worked over much. This smoothness is probably the outcome of Forster's relying on his letters and journal entries for the Gokul Ashtami festival, which comprises a good deal of "Temple." [16]

The exception, the pages Forster labored over longest, if the number of versions are any indication, is that part of chapter 36 which records the meeting between Aziz and Mrs. Moore's son Ralph. Thus, as with "Caves," the metaphysical material was pretty much formed in its creator's mind from the start, but problems begin to arise with the development of characters who will clarify the themes and the fabrication of action which will advance the plot—in the case of this chapter, with paralleling Aziz's original meeting with Mrs. Moore and getting Ralph and the doctor, total strangers, out of the guest

16. See Chapter 2, pp. 61–72.

house and onto the tank for the grand collision. Forster's solution, again like that of the Marabar scenes, is so carefully prepared that the reader accepts the pair's relationship and excursion as if they were the most natural developments in the world. To evoke Aziz's first meeting with Mrs. Moore at the mosque when the old lady emerged in the gloom from behind a pillar, Forster added to the MS's version of the encounter with Ralph the novel's sentence: "Something moved in the twilight of an adjoining room" (p. 308). In all versions, Aziz tells Ralph, "Then you are an Oriental," in response to the young man's assurance that he can always tell whether a stranger is his friend. These words, Forster reminds the reader, are the same ones Aziz spoke to Mrs. Moore under similar circumstances. In pursuing the notion that Ralph is a surrogate Mrs. Moore, Forster found the handle for moving the two men into the boat: Aziz would show Ralph the ritual as an act of homage to Mrs. Moore. In the MS, Forster had attempted to develop the idea that Ralph was worried about some vague danger menacing Stella on the water and wanted to take a boat out to see her. But the novelist abandoned this idea, most probably because it seemed unconvincing, and found, instead, in expanding the idea of Ralph's sharing his mother's intuitive approach to life, the means of furthering both plot and theme.

Forster's reintroduction in "Temple" of the phrase "then you are an Oriental" is consistent with an idea I believe he implemented late in the writing of *A Passage to India:* he determined to repeat and, if possible, expand in the novel's final section many of the motifs employed earlier in the book. Thus, in MS. A, Godbole, in his mystical state, recalls a lizard he may have met in the road (p. 360), rather than the novel's famous wasp seen perhaps on a stone (p. 286). The published work alone can claim to have incorporated fully the symbols of the

wasp and the stone into Forster's major theme of unity
and separation.[17] And when Aziz fears that he is beginning with Ralph another cycle of the friendship and
estrangement that he undertook with the English at the
novel's inception, only the novel, not any of the drafts,
uses the phrase "mosque, caves, mosque, caves" (p. 311)
to recapitulate the alternation of brotherhood and alienation symbolized by those places. Finally, only in the
published work does Fielding ask Aziz during their last
ride together if Godbole still says, "Come, come" (p. 319),
thus emphasizing in the novel's closing pages the motif
which, running through the book, epitomizes man's quest
for union with a spirit which transcends his isolated self.
Forster's conjunction of symbols parallels in method
"Temple's" substance: the attempted integration of
disparate elements.

There is one motif found in the MS which Forster
had thought of using in the last section of the book and
decided instead to drop; the little green bird with a red
bar on its wing that Adela and Ronny have seen during
the polo match pops up again when Fielding watches it
flit by during his ride with Aziz. Forster had previously
been unsure how much to develop the symbol of the bird.
In MS. A, Adela thinks about it after she and Ronny have
decided to become engaged, following their ride in the
nawab's car: "She remembered the bird that had watched
her from the tree—that Indian wild bird, possibly very
rare, whose name she would never know. And it seemed
to her that she was a bird, an unimportant one, shut up in
a cage with two perches labelled 'marriage' and 'not
marriage' and that she hopped from perch to perch in
order not to notice the cage" (p. 177). Here, the bird
symbolizes Adela's attempt to distract herself with labels
and roles in order to avoid contemplating the real

17. See Chapter 5, pp. 185-186.

problems of isolation and freedom. Forster omitted most of this idea, using in the novel, instead: "Unlike the green bird or the hairy animal, she was labelled now. She felt humiliated again, for she deprecated labels" (p. 94). Fielding, too, hates labels. In the novel, Forster writes of him: "To slink through India unlabelled was his aim" (p. 175). Perhaps this is the link that was to have connected the passages about the green bird, but Forster had another idea about labeling which he considered more important: no one can label India; she is too varied, too engulfing, for anyone to find the "real" India. This notion, which is ubiquitous in both the novel and the rough drafts, will be discussed more fully in the final chapter; here, I offer the suggestion that Forster abandoned the idea of the little green bird that, itself unlabeled, would remind Adela and Fielding that India had labeled them, because he was concerned not to weaken the novel's major argument against absolutes and essences: "Nothing embraces the whole of India, nothing, nothing" (p. 145).

The revisions in the plot and main themes of the novel having been examined, there remains to discuss the changes Forster made in regard to the published work's political and religious views, style, and characterization. In general, the alterations tend to sharpen the distinctions between ideas, make more vivid the Indian scene, and heighten the dramatic clashes between the characters.

The British in India are depicted more harshly in the novel; virtually every emendation is designed to make them appear less sympathetic. For example, in chapter 2, Hamidullah, Mahmoud Ali, and Aziz are chatting before dinner. Hamidullah says of the British who come out to India: "They all become exactly the same, not worse, not better. I give any Englishman two years, be he Turton or Burton. It is only the difference of a letter." Only in the novel, does he go on: "And I give any Englishwoman six months. All are exactly alike" (p. 11). Aside from the irony that an Englishwoman who is unlike any other, Mrs. Moore, has just arrived in Chandrapore, this addition reveals the hostility toward the Englishwoman in India which I have previously discussed in Chapter 2, pp. 33–34. Later in the same conversation, Hamidullah tells his guests that the son of a couple who treated him most kindly when he was a student in England is now in India; Hamidullah longs to see him, "but it is useless." Then the novel, not the MS, continues: "The other Anglo-Indians will have got hold of him long ago" (p. 12). Consistent with these changes, is the depiction of the surgeon, Major Callendar, as a fool and a bigot. While Aziz is having dinner in the scene I have been describing, the major sends for him. Forster records the Moslem's response only in the novel: "He has found out our dinner hour, that's all, and chooses to interrupt us every time, in order to show his power" (p. 15). When Ronny questions his mother about her meeting with Aziz, the novel adds to his "Did he seem to tolerate us—" the phrases "the brutal conqueror, the sundried bureaucrat, that sort of thing?" (p. 33). Ronny pities himself here as the butt of this self-portrayal, but the reader does not. Finally, many of Mrs. Turton's horrors are added to the novel, such as her remark at the Bridge Party that [the Indians] "ought never to have been allowed to drive in; it's so bad for them" (p. 41). The Anglo-Indian community accused Forster of sacrificing objectivity to score easy points in his novel, but there is evidence from other observers that his picture is substantially accurate. In any event, he was concerned with the novelist's task of presenting dramatically the confrontation of opposing camps.

This desire to offer the contrasting positions of all groups in India is what probably led Forster to expand

the material about the Christian missionaries which is in
a most sketchy condition in the drafts. In MS. A, chapter
4 leads from the penultimate paragraph dealing with the
circles of Indians who were beyond the reach of Turton's
Bridge Party invitation to the beginning of chapter 6:
"Aziz had not gone to the Bridge Party." The chapter
about the gathering itself was to be included elsewhere, but
the last paragraph of chapter 4, in which the Anglican
missionaries, Mr. Sorley and Mr. Graysford, address
themselves to the question of who gets into heaven—so
important to the major theme of the novel—appears only
in fragments of MS. B and appendix C, the latter a brief
addendum to MS. C. *B* contains the information that the
missionaries traveled third class, "slogged away at the
gospel of St. John," and believed that in my Father's
house are many mansions. Mr. Sorley here will admit into
heaven monkeys; he's not .sure about wasps; but no
plants, crystals, olives, air (p. 58). Appendix C is a bit
fuller: "Must the invitation proceed from Heaven? Old
Mr. Graysford thought so . . . which rendered him popular
among Hindus. And the jackals? Why not? The mercies
and the mysteries of God are infinite. And the wasps?
But Mr. Sorley became uneasy during the descent to
wasps, and when the vegetable kingdom was reached he
was apt to change the conversation" (p. 737). From these
bits and pieces, Forster created the chapter's wonderful,
final paragraph in which the theological wrestling of the
two divines is treated sympathetically—they are men of
good will and the problem is thorny—yet ultimately
condemned. Christianity does not offer the vision which
will make the universe one:

> All invitations must proceed from heaven perhaps;
> perhaps it is futile for men to initiate their own unity,
> they do but widen the gulfs between them by the attempt.
> So at all events thought old Mr. Graysford and young

Mr. Sorley, the devoted missionaries who lived out beyond the slaughterhouses, always travelled third on the railways, and never came up to the club. In our Father's house are many mansions, they taught, and there alone will the incompatible multitudes of mankind be welcomed and soothed. Not one shall be turned away by the servants on that verandah, be he black or white, not one shall be kept standing who approaches with a loving heart. And why should the divine hospitality cease here? Consider, with all reverence, the monkeys. May there not be a mansion for the monkeys also? Old Mr. Graysford said No, but young Mr. Sorley, who was advanced, said Yes; he saw no reason why monkeys should not have their collateral share of bliss, and he had sympathetic discussions about them with his Hindu friends. And the jackals? Jackals were indeed less to Mr. Sorley's mind, but he admitted that the mercy of God, being infinite, may well embrace all mammals. And the wasps? He became uneasy during the descent to wasps, and was apt to change the conversation. And oranges, cactuses, crystals and mud? and the bacteria inside Mr. Sorley? No, no, this is going too far. We must exclude someone from our gathering, or we shall be left with nothing. [pp. 37–38][18]

The final version of this material is a great improvement stylistically over its predecessors. Forster's ear, in this regard, is usually unerring and the novel would be far

18. Another passage about the missionaries which is introduced into the novel but which has no forerunner at all in the drafts concerns Aziz lying abed, ill, listening to the church bells: "It was Sunday, always an equivocal day in the East, and an excuse for slacking. He could hear church bells as he drowsed, both from the civil station and from the missionaries out beyond the slaughter house—different bells and rung with different intent, for one set was calling firmly to Anglo-India, and the other feebly to mankind. He did not object to the first set; the other he ignored, knowing their inefficiency. Old Mr. Graysford and young Mr. Sorley made converts during a famine, because they distributed food; but when times improved they were naturally left alone again, and though surprised and aggrieved each time this happened, they never learnt wisdom" (pp. 100–101).

more persuasive than the MS if no alterations other than those of style had been made. The opening lines of "Temple," for instance, employ the past tense in MS. A (p. 623), whereas in the novel, Forster writes: "Some hundreds of miles westward of the Marabar Hills, and two years later in time, Professor Narayan Godbole stands in the presence of God." With this simple change, the author not only sets his vivid scene before us with an immediacy only possible in the present tense, but creates the illusion that everything that has happened so far in the novel—the attempts at friendship, the estrangements after the expedition to the caves—everything has led up to this moment and will somehow be illuminated by it. Of course, not every small change produces such a large effect. Sometimes Forster just hits on a more felicitous phrase— in MS. A the servants "were piling provisions in the tonga" (p. 278), in the novel they "flung crockery" (p. 140)—but frequently he can energize the thrust of a satiric passage by the addition of a few telling images. For instance, Mrs. Blakiston who, as the wife of a small railway official, "was generally snubbed," appears in the MS, but as a much paler figure. In the scene in which the Anglo-Indians have gathered at the club to plot their strategy in response to Aziz's "assault" on Miss Quested, the members find themselves ironically rallying round the figure of Mrs. Blakiston as a much more appealing symbol of English womanhood than the meagre Adela, the actual victim of the alleged outrage. To this effect, Forster adds to Mrs. Blakiston in the novel "her abundant figure and masses of corn-gold hair," her wish that her baby would not spoil the high seriousness of the moment by blowing "bubbles down his chin," and her significance for the English: "[the women] moved out, subdued yet elated, Mrs. Blakiston in their midst like a sacred flame" (pp. 181, 182). Perhaps a comparison of two brief passages describing Aziz on the polo field will demonstrate most fully the sorts of small revisions Forster engaged in unceasingly to make his work more detailed, more natural, more vivid. In MS. A he writes:

> "Maharajah, salaam," called Aziz for a joke. The youths stopped and laughed. He told them not to exert themselves. They said they would not, and ran on.
> Riding into the middle, he began to knock the ball about. He could not play, but his pony could, and he set himself to learn, free from all human tensions. He forgot humanity as he scurried to and fro over the brown platter of the Maidan, with the evening wind on his forehead, and the encircling trees soothing his eyes. The ball shot away towards a subaltern who was also practising. [p. 99]

The published work offers the same lines with a few typical changes:

> "Maharajah, salaam," he called for a joke. The youths stopped and laughed. He advised them not to exert themselves. They promised they would not, and ran on.
> Riding into the middle, he began to knock the ball about. He could not play, but his pony could, and he set himself to learn, free from all human tension. He forgot the whole damned business of living as he scurried over the brown platter of the Maidan, with the evening wind on his forehead, and the encircling trees soothing his eyes. The ball shot away towards a stray subaltern who was also practising. [p. 57]

Although Forster retained the Hindu word *maidan* here, all his substitutions in the novel take the same direction: Indian words are translated into their less exotic English counterparts wherever clarity is at stake. Thus, *ghats* become "bathing steps," *khitmudgar* is transformed into "butler," and *gaddhi* is termed "throne."

Another aspect of the novel in which the revisions follow a completely consistent direction is the matter of the characters' backgrounds: in each case, the novel cuts out material about the pasts of the various people and leaves their histories much vaguer. Considering his characters particular enough, Forster moved in the direction of universalizing them.

Thus, Fielding is provided with a detailed past in MS. A. He has gone into partnership with an army coach in a boys' school, "hired a house on the edge of Dartmoor, and received backward youths at fancy prices." The partner's marriage to a neurotic woman causes all sorts of difficulty and Fielding sells his interest in the school. He then "goes on the loose with the proceeds." A brief "disreputable" phase ensues, followed by a "reaction." Here, Forster has crossed out "disgusted by his own vileness" and also "sinful nature." Fielding "regains equilibrium" and lives "to look back upon the period of repentance as far more dangerous than the excesses that have induced it"—for society has "approved" his self-revulsion. His money is now gone and since "he had stopped being ashamed, his father did not want to give him any more." Finally, the job as principal of Government College turns up and Fielding, nearly forty—a little younger than in the novel—arrives in Bombay (pp. 107–8). Forster, of course, does not in the novel replace this background with another; he merely boils it down to "His career, though scholastic, was varied, and had included going to the bad and repenting thereafter. . . . He did not mind whom he taught; public schoolboys, mental defectives and policemen had all come his way, and he had no objection to adding Indians" (p. 61).

As for the rest of Fielding's development in the novel as compared with the MS, there is no clear-cut pattern of change. Passages omitted from the drafts reveal the same concept of the character as paragraphs which appear only in the novel. In MS. B, Fielding "believed that the foreigner, though more difficult to reach than one's fellow countrymen, cannot be reached by different means: and sometimes, in the mental twilight, he knocked against an Indian who felt the same. Talk, he said openly, was a living force in the world: it was absurd to despise the vocal natives on the ground that they were not rich or well born or that what they were saying was not true. Why would people confuse a man's practical value with his moral?" (p. 114). The MS's Fielding is slightly different—harsher—in "Temple": "he had moved to the right in the last two years" (p. 709). He thinks, in B, "Aziz was lost to him—his sheet anchor amongst these people—and after two years he had ceased to mind. His marriage and other events were forcing him back to his natural caste. And here in the heart of Hindu-land, Aziz was not merely lost but unfamiliar, turned into something he would never have troubled to protect or cared to know" (p. 668). The novel's Fielding, though also grown more conservative, is kinder and more affectionate than this. His marriage makes him seem more youthful to the reader at the same time that it makes Fielding seem older to himself. The MS, again offering more background, sheds some light on the history of Fielding's relationship with Stella: "His sudden wooing of Stella had been a reaction from the East. He was not quite happy about his marriage. His wife was inexperienced and beautiful and he had caught her before she had had a chance [in one version, Fielding is "ashamed of catching her so young, fresh from her convent"] . . . in reaction from the death of her mother" (p. 705). This material is implied in the novel.

As with Fielding, Aziz is granted a past history in the original drafts which the published work leaves out. He has been a medical student in Germany and recites at

Hamidullah's a poem by Heine instead of the works by Moslem poets that he quotes in the novel.[19] He has fenced in Germany and now did exercises every morning. But unlike Fielding's, Aziz's personality undergoes a subtle evolution during the creation of *A Passage to India.* He becomes more rebellious, more volatile, more Moslem. In the novel, as opposed to the drafts, he refuses to clean his teeth before leaving Hamidullah's to see Major Callendar (p. 17). In MS. A, when Aziz notices Mesdames Lesley and Callendar at the major's house, he "stood back respectfully" (p. 18). He does not do so in the novel. And, in the novel, he at first treats Mrs. Moore more severely during their encounter in the mosque, telling her, "You have no right here at all" (p. 20). His outburst in this scene against the Englishwomen who have just snubbed him is also stronger in the novel, yet only in the published version do Aziz and Mrs. Moore sit down side-by-side to replace their shoes, thus giving the meeting a more dramatic sense of reconciliation.

The relationship between Aziz and his former wife is developed much more fully in the novel giving the reader a clearer understanding of his sensitivity and sensuality. Indeed, all of the characters are rounder in the book than in the drafts. Adela, Ronny, Collector Turton, the Nawab

19.   Vergiftet sind meine Lieder
       Wie könnt' es anders sein?
       Du hast mir ja Gift gegossen
       Ins blühende Leben hinein.

       Vergiftet sind meine Lieder,
       Wie könnt' es anders sein?
       Ich trage im Herzen viel Schlangen,
       Und dich, Geliebte mein.

The poem shares certain qualities with those poems Aziz admires in the novel: chief amongst these is pathos, but the imagery of the blooming garden of life and the poisonous snakes of the heart must also have been congenial to him. Nevertheless, in Sufi poems of the type Aziz recites later in the novel, the beloved is treated far more gently.

Bahadur, even Godbole are more completely realized. But it is by modifying Mrs. Moore's character that Forster most strengthened a weak spot in his original conception.

In the rough drafts, Mrs. Moore is a commonplace old lady, orthodox and unimpressive. She offers no contrast to Adela's literalness, Fielding's rationalism, Aziz's emotionality or Godbole's tranquility. She is merely Miss Quested's companion and confidante. But Forster gradually changes her blandness into a vulnerability so great that when her black vision arrives it colors much of the book. Against this pessimistic view or, rather, at an angle to it, he imposes Godbole's conviction, and these two sides of the metaphysical question create the tension which continues to support *A Passage to India* years after its political relevance has given way.

In MS. A, Mrs. Moore is "considered by herself and the younger generation as a rather negligible old lady" (p. 29). She is uninterested in trying to comprehend India, not because she thinks it unfathomable, but because she has already used up all her energy in liking or disliking people. Adela tells her that she is "quaint" and they both laugh (pp. 34, 31). When the younger woman is terribly upset because no one is showing her the "real" India, only in the novel does Forster describe Mrs. Moore as wiser than Adela. Mrs. Moore "did not take the disappointment as seriously as Miss Quested, for the reason that she was forty years older, and had learnt that Life never gives us what we want at the moment that we consider appropriate. Adventures do occur, but not punctually" (p. 25). In MS. A, Fielding finds her lacking in dignity during the tea party: "Mrs. Moore, of whom he had hopes, proved no better than the rest. Going round the college with him, she had been shallow and distrait, and now rivalled Aziz himself in garrulity, joining Miss Quested and tacking hither and thither for her farewells

with Miss Quested in her wake" (p. 141). Even at the
Marabar, the Mrs. Moore of MS. A is silly: "Caves are
dangerous for old women—I mean for a feeble old woman
like me" (p. 304).

In the novel, Mrs. Moore grows in two dimensions:
besides her increased stature, her Christianity widens into
mysticism. The first hint of this change occurs in the
conversation with Adela and Ronny about the dead
bodies floating down the Ganges. In MS. A, it is Adela
who is unnerved by the information that the muggers eat
corpses. Mrs. Moore's opinion is "I don't see why the
muggers shouldn't eat them." In another early version,
although she is bothered by the idea that crocodiles are
down in the beautiful river, her attitude toward the fate
of the bodies is still matter of fact (pp. 48–50). In sharp
contrast with this reasonableness is Mrs. Moore's response
in the novel:

> The dead bodies floated down that way from Benares,
> or would if the crocodiles let them. "It's not much of a
> dead body that gets down to Chandrapore," [said
> Ronny].
> "Crocodiles down in it too, how terrible!" his mother
> murmured. The young people glanced at each other and
> smiled; it amused them when the old lady got these
> gentle creeps, and harmony was restored between them
> consequently. She continued: "What a terrible river!
> what a wonderful river!" and sighed. [p. 32]

Here it is Adela who is commonsensical and Mrs. Moore
who is awed by the lovely, frightening Indian river. Such
a woman as is depicted here could encounter an overwhelming truth in a Marabar Cave—and not deny or
subvert it. But the character as conceived in the earlier
drafts is closed to such experiences. When Adela and
Ronny tell her about the accident in the nawab's car and
the old man's supernatural explanation of the incident,

she replies primly in MS. A: "No, I don't believe in ghosts, I don't know how those of us who call ourselves Christian can" (p. 188). But, in the novel, her response is diametrically opposite: "Mrs. Moore shivered, 'A ghost!' But the idea of a ghost scarcely passed her lips. The young people did not take it up, being occupied with their own outlooks, and deprived of support it perished, or was reabsorbed into the part of the mind that seldom speaks" (p. 97). Here, it is the old lady who brings up the idea that the accident was occasioned by a departed spirit. In the published work, Mrs. Moore is intuitive throughout, and always close to mystical states. This is the sort of character whom the Hindus can themselves deify; after her death, Mrs. Moore becomes a process and a presence. Her troubled spirit, along with the wasp that she admired, is absorbed by Godbole and transformed into a hopeful surge toward union with God.

Mrs. Moore's character has presented great difficulties to the novel's critics. One of the advantages of having an edition of Forster's manuscripts available is the wealth of new evidence that students of the novel will now possess to aid their deliberations. And of chief importance amongst the evidence is, I think, the altered concept of Mrs. Moore. From a feeble old lady whose collapse in a railway carriage is at best a side issue, Forster has transformed her into an idealist become disillusionment incarnate. In this capacity, she is a perfect counterpoise to Professor Godbole's cheerful mysticism—a balance which Adela in her pathological condition, Fielding in his atheistic humanism, Aziz in his indifference to cosmology cannot effect. Yet the manuscripts and text show Forster consistently lending more weight to the abysmal cave and the radiant temple as equal measures on the scale of values with which the novel is primarily concerned.

4. *A Passage to India* and the Critics

WRITING ABOUT the current boom in Melville criticism, E. M. Forster observes that "like all plowed-up authors his surface has got rather bumpy." [1] Forster himself was almost virgin terrain for two decades after the publication of *A Passage to India*, but, since the years of the Second World War, he has been cultivated by a crowd of diggers, and the dust has not settled yet.

In the twenties and thirties, Forster was usually accorded some attention in studies of the English novel or commentaries on the literary scene, [2] but sustained, serious

---

1. E. M. Forster, "*The Enchafed Flood*," review of *The Enchafed Flood* by W. H. Auden, in *Two Cheers for Democracy* (New York: Harcourt, Brace & Co., 1951), p. 267. This review first appeared in 1951. Although some works have been cited previously, all works mentioned in this chapter will be cited again in full.

2. See, for example, Elizabeth Drew, *The Modern Novel* (New York: Harcourt, Brace & Co., 1926); Bonamy Dobree, *The Lamp and the Lute* (London: Clarendon Press, 1929); Q. D. Leavis, *Fiction and the Reading Public* (London: Chatto & Windus, 1932); Frank Swinnerton, *The Georgian Literary Scene* (London: Hutchinson & Co., 1939); and Dorothy M. Hoare, *Some Studies in the Modern Novel* (Philadelphia: Dufour Editions, 1953).

criticism was rare.[3] Then, during the forties, Forster was found relevant to a wartorn society. J. C. Ransom, in an article partly occasioned by the publication of Lionel Trilling's *E. M. Forster* (1943),[4] speaks of a Forster "revival" which he finds further evidenced by Knopf's reissue of *Where Angels Fear to Tread* and *Howards End* and New Directions' new editions of *The Longest Journey* and *A Room With a View*.[5] Following this wave, interest in Forster seems to have ebbed slightly until the appearance of James McConkey's excellent book, *The Novels of E. M. Forster* (1957).[6] Frederick P. W. McDowell attributes this pause in the flow to the respect given Trilling's authoritative study.[7] But, with the publication of McConkey's book,

3. The sole full length study of Forster during this period is Rose Macaulay, *The Writings of E. M. Forster* (London: Harcourt, Brace & Co., 1938). The chief shorter studies are Edward Shanks, "Mr. E. M. Forster," *London Mercury* XVI (July 1927), 265–74; Virginia Woolf, "The Novels of E. M. Forster," *Atlantic Monthly* CXL (November 1927), 642–48; I. A. Richards, "A Passage to Forster," *Forum* LXXVIII (December 1927), 914–20; Howard N. Doughty, Jr., "The Novels of E. M. Forster," *Bookman* LXXV (October 1932), 542–49; Montgomery Belgion, "The Diabolism of Mr. E. M. Forster," *Criterion* XIV (October 1934), 54–73; Peter Burra, "The Novels of E. M. Forster," *Nineteenth Century and After* CXVI (November 1934), 581–94; F. R. Leavis, "E. M. Forster," *Scrutiny* VII (September 1938), 185–202; and a section of Reuben Brower, *The Fields of Light* (New York: Oxford University Press, 1951), pp. 182–98. Of these, the analyses of Brower and Burra are found most interesting and useful today. Belgion, the most unsympathetic of Forster's critics, is noteworthy for hostility rather than cogency.

4. Lionel Trilling, *E. M. Forster* (New York: New Directions, 1943).

5. J. C. Ransom, "E. M. Forster," *Kenyon Review* V (Autumn 1943), 403. See also E. K. Brown, "The Revival of E. M. Forster," *Yale Review* XXXII (Summer 1944), 668–81. The latter essay has been reprinted in *Forms of Modern Fiction*, ed. William Van O'Connor (Minneapolis: University of Minnesota Press, 1948).

6. James McConkey, *The Novels of E. M. Forster* (Ithaca, N.Y.: Cornell University Press, 1957).

7. Frederick P. W. McDowell, "The Newest Elucidations of Forster," *English Fiction in Transition* V, no. 4 (1962), 351.

Forster criticism has flooded the field and continues to rise.[8]

One of the trends in recent criticism of *A Passage to India* has been the greater stress critics have afforded the work's philosophic import to the exclusion of devoting attention to the historic situation the novel treats. Earlier commentators, closer to the world of the British Raj, were more concerned with Forster's political and social views than with his metaphysics. Those writers who offered topical interpretations were not oblivious to the Hindu and Moslem material in the book, but they were often caught up in the debate about imperialism which is no longer a live issue.

On June 2, 1926, Forster's good friend and mentor, G. Lowes Dickinson, wrote the novelist about his reactions to *A Passage to India*, which he had just finished reading. Dickinson states his conception of the theme firmly: "the incompatibility of Indians and English," and he praises Forster for "understanding both sides"—yet he is not sure this is what the novelist is really after; he feels "all

political

8. Aside from a large number of articles, six other books on Forster have appeared in the past decade: J. H. Oliver, *The Art of E. M. Forster* (Melbourne: Melbourne University Press, 1960); K. W. Grandsen, *E. M. Forster* (New York: Grove Press, 1962); Frederick C. Crews, *E. M. Forster: The Perils of Humanism* (Princeton: Princeton University Press, 1962); J. B. Beer, *The Achievement of E. M. Forster* (London: Chatto & Windus, 1963); Alan Wilde, *Art and Order: A Study of E. M. Forster* (New York: New York University Press, 1964); and Wilfred Stone, *The Cave and the Mountain* (Stanford: Stanford University Press, 1966). Rex Warner, *E. M. Forster* (London, 1950), has been revised by John Morris and reprinted in the British Writers and Their Work Series (Lincoln: University of Nebraska Press, 1964); Harry T. Moore has published a monograph, *E. M. Forster*, in the Columbia Essays on Modern Writers Series (New York: Columbia University Press, 1965); and *Forster: A Collection of Critical Essays* has been edited by Malcolm Bradbury for the Twentieth Century Views Series (Englewood Cliffs, N.J.: Prentice-Hall, 1966). This period has also seen new editions or printings of Forster's five novels, collected stories, two travel guides, two collections of essays, and study of the novel.

sorts of behind suggestions," as if Forster has "lifted a new corner of the veil." But then he shrugs off these speculations and asks, "What did happen in the Caves?" [9] Many of his contemporaries agreed with Dickinson's assessment of the theme; modern critics might concede that British-Indian relations form the subject, at least, of the book, but their emphasis is different. Phyllis Bentley, who was writing in the period of turbulence which marked India's independence from Britain and separation from Pakistan, conceives of the novel completely in political terms: "Its theme is that conqueror and conquered cannot be friends; the relationship is wrong from the start, whether between individuals or nations, and must be destroyed before any good relationship can be attempted." [10] A few years later, Arnold Kettle, a Marxist critic who also stresses the political side of the book, wrote in partial agreement with Miss Bentley that the novel's subject is raised during the dinner party at Hamidullah's: "Whether or not it is possible to be friends with an Englishman." Kettle believes that Forster's answer is given at the end of the work: "No, not yet, no, not here." But he does not like Forster's generalizing on the basis of the Aziz-Fielding relationship. He thinks that if Fielding had been prepared to renounce further "the imperialistic attitude" the friendship might have gone further. [11] One of the few critics writing today who stress the historical aspect of *A Passage to India*, Benita Parry, thinks that Forster calls for both political and spiritual regeneration: "The book has a deep social and historical sense; the clash of cultures is firmly

9. E. M. Forster, *Goldsworthy Lowes Dickinson* (New York: Harcourt, Brace & Co., 1934), pp. 215, 216.

10. Phyllis Bentley, "The Novels of E. M. Forster," *College English* IX (April 1948), 354.

11. Arnold Kettle, *An Introduction to the English Novel*, 2 vols. (London: Hutchinson's Universal Library, 1953), I:153, 159. Perhaps Forster felt that when a system can only be circumvented by actions more heroic than Fielding's, it is the system rather than the man which must be reexamined.

placed, in the historical situation of a British Raj ruling a subject people at a particular point in time; cultural and political as well as spiritual matters are fully explored by the action; and if East and West are in any way to meet, then Forster considers a change in the external relations between them to be quite as necessary as a revolution in man's restricted spiritual and human responses." [12]

Some of the critics who view the novel as an interpretation of political history have attacked the accuracy or the soundness of Forster's presentation. In 1927, in an article in the *London Mercury*, Edward Shanks scolded Forster for exaggerating Anglo-Indian folly. Shanks, who is obviously no Aristotelian, complains that Forster treats the possible as if it were probable: "I am told by persons who are likely to know that Mr. Forster does exaggerate what he seems to find wrong in the attitude of the British. The plot does seem to me, ignorant as I am of Indian conditions, to show traces of those exaggerations which are natural but not permissible to the novelist—I mean events which might have happened presented as if they must have happened. The English community of Chandrapore might have been consistently hostile to the natives as it is here shown to be: probably it was not." [13] Shanks is one of the few readers of *A Passage to India* to object that Fielding is an authorial mouthpiece rather than a developed character. Furthermore, Shanks believes that Forster should eschew a discussion of politics in the book since he obviously has strong opinions on the subject:

> Mr. Forster has between his English and his Indians a sort of *raisonneur*, one Fielding, principal of the College at Chandrapore, who takes his middle place between the two races with a more conspicuous want of tact than

12. Benita Parry, "Passage to More Than India," in *Forster: A Collection of Critical Essays*, p. 160. The essay appeared for the first time in this collection, edited by Bradbury (1966).

13. Edward Shanks, "Mr. E. M. Forster," p. 272.

suits the scheme of the book—unless the author had
wished, as apparently he does not, to satirise the dis-
comforts of the mediator. . . .

Fielding does nearly spoil the book because his
running commentary on the racial problems raised (and,
save in isolated moments, he is rather a running commentary than a person) gives it more of the air of a
political argument than it should have had. For such a
dispute Mr. Forster is not fitted: if he attempted it his
impartiality would doom it from the beginning to
inconclusiveness.[14]

Another critic, D. S. Savage, scores Forster, not for
satirizing British officialdom in India, but for ignoring the
basis of British power. "One is reminded of his treatment
of the 'Indian question' in his fifth and last novel, where
the ugly realities underlying the presence of the British in
India are not even glanced at, and the issues raised are
handled as though they could be solved on the surface
level of personal intercourse and individual behaviour."[15]

Writers with political biases different from Savage's have
also found the book's chief interest to be in the development of Forster's thoughts about India rather than its
artistic merits. Frank Swinnerton writes: "*A Passage to
India* is less interesting as a novel than as a presentation, a
crystallization, of Forster's thoughts and emotions after
two long exploratory visits to the East. He does not like
British rule; it is in the hands of Conventionalists. However, he has some doubts as to the consequences of its

14. Ibid.
15. D. S. Savage, *The Withered Branch* (London: Eyre & Spottiswoode,
1950), p. 47. A Marxist critic, Savage despises Forster's brand of democracy.
He also oversimplifies Forster's faith in the efficacy of personal relations.
Forster wrote home, in 1921, that "good manners" cannot "avert a political
upheaval. But they can minimize it. . . . But it's too late. Indians don't long
for social intercourse with Englishmen any longer." (*The Hill of Devi* [New
York: Harcourt, Brace & Co., 1953], p. 237). This comes close to expressing
the complex attitude revealed in the novel.

abandonment. In this conclusion, having been a Liberal, he becomes a philosopher, and leaves everything where he found it." [16] The chief attack on the politics of *A Passage to India* does not come from an Englishman of any persuasion, but from a Hindu, Nirad C. Chaudhuri, who finds something wrong with everything in the book. First of all, the novel contains nothing of the conflict between Indian nationalists and the British administration (which was, if not "the largest sector of Indo-British relation," as Chaudhuri asserts, certainly a very important area, but one about which Forster knew little). Chaudhuri charges that the book deals only with the conflict "between associates, the British officials and their Indian subordinates or hangers-on." And Chaudhuri is scathing in his denunciation of administrators and hangers-on: "Both the groups of characters in *A Passage to India* are insignificant and despicable. . . . Aziz would not have been allowed to cross my threshold, not to speak of being taken as an equal. . . . [He] and his friends belong to the servile sector and are all inverted toadies." Then again, the Hindu characters, because they are modeled on types found mostly in the Princely States are so traditional that they do not represent modern India at all: "To those of us who are familiar with the teachings of Hindu reformers of the 19th century, Godbole is not an exponent of Hinduism, he is a clown." Another mistake Forster makes is in using Moslems as the second party in the British-Indian relationship. Although he needs a Hindu protagonist, Forster does not create one because he "shares the liking the British in India had for the Muslim, and the corresponding dislike for the Hindu." This incredible statement will come as a shock to most of Forster's readers, but Chaudhuri strikes closer to home with other remarks, even though his assumptions are different from Forster's. He

16. Frank Swinnerton, *The Georgian Literary Scene*, p. 319.

agrees with Savage about "the book's tacit but confident assumption that Indo-British relations presented a problem of personal behaviour and could be tackled on a personal plane. They did not and could not." What Chaudhuri wants is an entirely different book, "a tragedy of mutual repulsion and not a tragi-comedy of mutual attraction." Forster's irony is anathema to him: the novel "shows a great imperial system at its worst, not as diabolically evil but as drab and asinine; the rulers and the ruled alike are depicted at their smallest, the snobbery and pettiness of the one matching the imbecility and rancour of the other." But Chaudhuri does not want a dissolution of the Anglo-Indian relationship: the British influence "could have been providential if the English were not selfish." Ironically, he thinks India had more to gain by being the recipient of British science and culture than Forster does. Despite, or because of, its overheated tone, Chaudhuri's essay emphasizes Forster's own calm, tolerant detachment; however, the Hindu's passion is not without the ability to move one to question Forster's habitual understatement, as when Chaudhuri laments that, in the novel, "Our suffering under British rule . . . is deprived of all dignity."[17]

A large number of critics, among the most articulate of whom is D. J. Enright, have taken the position that *A Passage to India* "is a good deal more than a political novel; and even in its political aspect, it is a good deal more than Indians versus Englishmen or the pros and cons of colonialism. For what *is* India? Not a neat little unit like Switzerland or Monaco, but a vast expanse of changing countryside and a vast mass of differing races, religions, and customs. . . . India [is] something which can hardly be conceived of."[18] These writers have seen the

17. Nirad C. Chaudhuri, "Passage to and from India," *Encounter* II (June 1954), pp. 20, 21, 22, 23.

18. D. J. Enright, *The Apothecary's Shop: Essays on Literature* (Philadelphia: Dufour Editions, 1957), p. 176.

historical setting as Forster's means of probing a universal condition, rather than as an end in itself: Morton Dauwen Zabel writes, "The political situation is only an external aspect of the deep seated moral situation which is Forster's real concern."[19] Even Lionel Trilling, who writes from within the historical-social tradition of literary criticism, concludes his chapter on Forster's last novel with a statement about the work's wide significance: "Great as the problem of India is, Forster's book is not about India alone; it is about all of human life."[20] A similar view is expressed by George H. Thomson: "India reflects all the world and all its people."[21] Frederick C. Crews carries this notion even further; he holds that India is the principal figure in the novel and, could she be fathomed, all creation would be comprehensible: "The image of India as a whole is more important than any of the figures, English or Indian, who move across it. To understand India is to understand the rationale of the whole creation; but the characters do not understand it, and Forster's plot makes us ask whether human faculties are capable of such understanding at all."[22]

umm, → apparently this criticus capable

One would expect that many writers would have essayed an appraisal of Forster as social critic and satirist, but very few have even touched on the matter. Perhaps this is because the comedy of the earlier novels, especially the first three, has been analyzed, and explicators want to treat the serious philosophical issues in *A Passage to*

19. Morton Dauwen Zabel, *Craft and Character in Modern Fiction* (New York: Viking Press, 1957), p. 243. See also Warner's *E. M. Forster:* "But the book is much more than a study of the British Raj, more even than a study of the difficulties attending on personal relationships. It is Forster's most philosophical novel" (p. 24).

20. Trilling, *E. M. Forster*, p. 161.

21. George H. Thomson, "Thematic Symbol in *A Passage to India*," *Twentieth Century Literature* VII (July 1961), 52.

22. Crews, *The Perils of Humanism*, p. 144.

India. Perhaps Forster's talents in this direction are taken for granted and critics want to turn to more controversial subjects. In any event, little has been published on the success with which Forster hits his targets in the novel. One Anglo-Indian and early commentator, E. A. Horne, who is friendly to Forster and, like him, hostile to British imperialists, holds that the book's English people do not always ring true. He thinks Forster went out to the subcontinent to get to know Indians and learned about Anglo-Indians from them. Paraphrasing Fielding's advice to Adela in the novel, he suggests that Forster should have tried seeing Anglo-Indians to write about them. Horne does confirm the British attitude toward the playing of the national anthem that Forster describes in the novel, as well as the scene in which Aziz's tonga is appropriated by two English ladies, and the accuracy of Forster's description of the Anglo-Indian distaste for art.[23] Chaudhuri attacks the treatment of the British more vigorously. He thinks Forster ridicules them for the wrong reason: "The shortcoming of the British official was not in courage, but in intelligence."[24] Enright is more tentative than Chaudhuri and more inclined to accept Forster's presentation: "Does he caricature the British officials? Even allowing for the artificiality of their manner of living, their reactions to the Aziz case are in the worst tradition of melodrama.... It *is* a little difficult to believe that government officials could behave with such unanimous stupidity—but Chandrapore was a long time ago, and perhaps, like the rest of us, even officials are tending to improve these days."[25] Despite the writers quoted, Forster's social comedy in *A Passage to India* appears to be an area neglected in favor of the novel's metaphysical import.

23. E. A. Horne, "Mr. Forster's *A Passage to India,*" *New Statesman* LVI (September 6, 1958), 544.

24. Chaudhuri, "Passage to and from India," p. 21.

25. Enright, *The Apothecary Shop*, pp. 181, 182.

The bent of recent criticism is toward a symbolic analysis of *A Passage to India* to the exclusion of the social and political concerns of earlier commentators. Malcolm Bradbury writes of this new direction: "The balance of criticism has now turned so far in favour of regarding Forster as a modern symbolist that we are sometimes in danger of forgetting the important fact about him that many earlier critics never got beyond—that he is a comic social novelist, . . . a man who manifests and is attentive to the social and historical context out of which he derives. This is not the whole Forster, but it is a Forster who never ceases to be present in all the novels, short stories, travel books, and essays."[26]

A survey of the novel's criticism is overdue: of the issues it has formulated and the clarifications it has offered. One important question has already been discussed, that is, whether *A Passage to India* is primarily a social and political novel, treating Anglo-Indian relations through the medium of satire, in which case the appositeness of Forster's presentation and the quality of his political commitment are matters of great consequence, or whether it is primarily a philosophical novel, transcending topicality to explore the metaphysical significance of certain states of existence which India symbolizes. Perhaps the major issue, the problem which seems to subsume the greatest number of difficulties, and about which there is far from universal agreement, is whether *A Passage to India* reveals a pessimistic or optimistic view of the universe. Related to this question are speculation about the book's structure, interpretations of the "Caves" and "Temple" sections, and evaluations of the role played by rationalism and mysticism. The final question around which a body of discussion has cohered is whether the book's realistic plane is too detached from its symbolic

26. Bradbury, Introduction, *Forster: Critical Essays*, p. 3.

level. While there is controversy about Forster's success in combining these two disparate aspects, most critics have taken Forster's skill as a social critic for granted and gone on to explicate his symbols, often with helpful results.

It may seem incredible that readers of *A Passage to India* have been unable to agree whether Forster's conclusion is that life is more joyous than bleak or more bleak than joyous; nevertheless, as Bradbury observes, "Nobody has yet resolved even the divergent accounts available of the meaning of *A Passage to India*. Is it—the case may be simply put—a novel which, after attempting to reconcile the differences between races, religions, social creeds, nature and man, asserts failure?—or is it a novel which, reaching beyond accepted faiths and accepted interpretations of the mysterious, the unseen, asserts a positive vision of unity? Is Forster . . . a spiritual and social optimist; or are his conclusions those of pessimism and defeat?"[27] An examination of the themes found by many critics indicates that the balance is tipped in favor of an optimistic Forster, but a convinced and sizable minority dissents—and a number of mixed verdicts further unsettles the weight of opinion. Among the scholars who find *A Passage to India* affirmative in its views, several positions can be ascertained. One group contents itself with presenting the idea that Forster's is, by and large, a hopeful view of the universe. A second group particularizes this notion and says that the novel posits order in creation. Narrowing the range still further, some critics find that unity is the underlying factor in Forster's conception of the universe, while others believe Forster holds a dualistic philosophy. Of course, all of these ideas are not mutually exclusive and some writers can be found in more than one camp.

Most of the critics who discover in Forster a persistent,

27. Ibid., pp. 13–14.

if vague, affirmation stress the positive values he holds and
the struggle he endorses to support them. In Elizabeth
Hamill's view, his passionate concern is "to point out that
there is a Truth, a Way and a Life which we constantly
miss or falsify by hypocrisy, conventional humbug and
dreary muddle."[28] Zabel also sees Forster as a moral
crusader who is constantly exhorting man to attempt, at
least, to triumph over the internal and external evils that
assail him, but he is much more sanguine than Hamill
about Forster's conviction that man can win the battle.[29]
Barbara Hardy, another critic who admits that Forster
has created in his novel an effective symbolization of evil,
also agrees with Zabel that the evil is routed. She writes:
"Forster is pushing his intransigent material as far as he
can in the direction of optimistic hope. The anti-vision
is chiefly there, it seems to me, so that it shall be powerfully
withdrawn."[30] Critics of this persuasion often feel that
Forster's commitment to love as a healing force is the
vision he opposes to his gloomy appraisal of the strength
of the destructive element. Enright is one of these; he
finds that in *A Passage to India* the novelist is "at his best
and firmest—neither cynic nor sentimentalist: one who
believes in love, but doubts whether it will ever quite
drive out fear and hatred."[31] If the views attributed to
Forster seem to present a rather restricted affirmation, it
should be understood that this group of critics sees
Forster as having gone beyond an acknowledgment of the
presence of evil in the world to formulate an antidote.
According to Bradbury, "In all his novels, but particularly in the two last, one is aware of an urgent attempt

28. Elizabeth Hamill, *These Modern Writers* (Melbourne: Georgian
House, 1946), p. 139.

29. Zabel, *Craft and Character in Modern Fiction*, pp. 228–52.

30. Barbara Hardy, *The Appropriate Form: An Essay on the Novel* (London:
Athlone Press, University of London, 1964), p. 78.

31. Enright, *The Apothecary's Shop*, p. 186.

to achieve some kind of reconciling and poetic vision, to approach through emotion, through the developed heart, those sensations of body and spirit that not only create a full life in the living but give a meaning to life, afford a visionary understanding of it." [32]

That Forster believes order underlies the universe is easier to intuit than to demonstrate, partly because order is, by its own nature, hard to pin down. E. K. Brown, deservedly one of the most influential of Forster's interpreters, believes that "the main effect in *A Passage to India* is . . . of order in the universe, but order that can be merely glimpsed, never seized for sure." [33] The critics who have defended this view most successfully are those who, like Brown, have used the highly organized structure of *A Passage to India* itself as the basis for their claim that Forster means the novel's aesthetic plan to reflect an order in the world of men and gods. James McConkey, in substantial agreement with Brown, thinks that the cyclic movement of the work implies an ordering pattern: at the end of the novel when "we sense the beginning of a new cycle . . . we sense the order beyond the cycle." [34] For Glen O. Allen, this ordering principle is most clearly expressed in an idea found in *Howards End:* "Proportion is the final secret." [35] For other critics, Barbara Hardy among them, the idea of order in the universe is more a need expressed through the novel than an actuality manifested in it: "The pressure toward order is its weakness." [36] Although relatively few commentators have addressed themselves to this problem directly, the patterns

32. Bradbury, Introduction, *Forster: Critical Essays*, p. 6.

33. E. K. Brown, *Rhythm in the Novel* (Toronto: University of Toronto Press, 1950), p. 114.

34. McConkey, *The Novels of E. M. Forster*, p. 13.

35. Glen O. Allen, "Structure, Symbol, and Theme in *A Passage to India*," *PMLA* LXX (December 1955), 954.

36. Hardy, *The Appropriate Form*, p. 80.

that critics have found in the book and the concepts that they believe these patterns symbolize in Forster's cosmology suggest that there is a more general conviction of Forster's allegiance to the idea of universal order than is usually acknowledged.

Critics who assert that Forster's main concern in the novel is with order tend to dwell on metaphysical problems. Those who think that Forster's subject is unity emphasize the human dimension. Thus, Richard M. Kain writes: "Throughout his career as a novelist, Forster's dominant theme has been that of the attainment of harmonious union, whether between personalities, social groups, or contrasting ideas and attitudes."[37] Richard J. Voorhees puts the matter even more succinctly: "The problem with which *A Passage to India* mainly deals [is] the problem of human unity."[38] Many commentators believe that Forster is advocating the value and feasibility of human unity even as he shows the enormous difficulties that attend its realization. McConkey is one of the few critics who discuss unity in terms of Forster's desire to achieve union with some force outside of the world of men. Forster, he contends, is "a writer most keenly aware of discord and lack of harmony in his world who nevertheless senses, however obscurely, a harmony beyond and strives for identification with it."[39]

A number of critics have attempted to comprehend both aspects of Forster—the social realist and the advocate of the unseen—in their appraisals. Stuart Hampshire describes this dualism most exactly:

37. Richard M. Kain, "Vision and Discovery in E. M. Forster's *A Passage to India*," in *Twelve Original Essays in Great English Novels*, ed. Charles Shapiro (Detroit: Wayne State University Press, 1960), p. 257.

38. Richard J. Voorhees, "The Novels of E. M. Forster," *South Atlantic Quarterly* LIII (January 1954), 90.

39. McConkey, *The Novels of E. M. Forster*, p. 92. See also Stone, *The Cave and the Mountain*: "[The novel] is Forster's greatest effort to relate the broken arcs of his own experience to some final scheme of ultimate value" (p. 299).

An underlying argument, a division of allegiance, runs through all of Mr. Forster's writing and shapes the developing style and structure of his novels. Roughly stated, the division is between, on the one side, an inherited liberalism confirmed among lifelong friends at Cambridge and never altogether discarded, which stressed the authority of the individual conscience, and stressed also the qualities of sensitiveness and lucidity in personal relations within the setting of a civilized private life. On the other side, Mr. Forster has always represented the natural order surrounding this little compound of cultivated ground as sublime, unknown, unlimited, and as not adapted to our powers of understanding. We cannot be safe and at home within the compound, however much we may defensively pretend to be. The function of art is to take men outside the compound of conscious awareness, beyond their moral anxieties, and to find expression for the deeper rhythms in nature from which we are otherwise disconnected."[40]

No matter which polarity is stressed—reason-feeling, individualism-Communalism, realism-symbolism—Forster's inconclusiveness, his refusal to mediate among the significant possibilities of experience, has impressed many readers. In connection with this inconclusiveness, McConkey writes, "Forster's interest in both the human and transcendent realities accounts for what his friend G. Lowes Dickinson has termed his kind of 'double vision,' a sense of 'this world, and a world or worlds behind.' These 'worlds behind' cannot be ignored or given a minor position by the critic, for in Forster the sense of the transcendent realm consistently affects and colors the physical realm."[41] The "double vision" allows for a dual interpretation of the novel's theme. Walter Allen describes two

40. Stuart Hampshire, "Two Cheers for Mr. Forster," *New York Review of Books* VI (May 12, 1966), 194. Reprinted from *The New York Review of Books*. Copyright © 1966 by *The New York Review*.

41. McConkey, *The Novels of E. M. Forster*, p. 3.

planes in the book: on the plane of realism, no reconciliation is possible, but, on the metaphysical plane, reconciliation can and does take place.[42] Glen Pedersen subscribes to much the same view: "The literal level of the novel emphasizes the divisions between the Indians and the Englishmen, the diversity among men; the symbolic level reveals the way to union and unity."[43]

Although the critics who have been cited thus far have rarely found Forster an unmitigated optimist, they have judged that *A Passage to India* expresses a positive vision and the possibility, at least, of man's approaching it. The opposing opinion—that Forster's vision is negative and that the universe reveals no order or unity—has also found supporters. That Forster shared Eliot's view of modern life as a wasteland of despair and disillusionment—Eliot's poem was published two years before *A Passage to India*—has been suggested by some critics.[44] One of the recent writers on Forster most insistent on the novelist's gloom, Alan Wilde, believes that "Forster's disillusionment spreads over a larger area than usual: there is a breakdown in his last novel of communication of every kind, and the life of the body becomes as suspect as the life of the mind."[45] Wilde sees the novel as setting forth a universe characterized by disorder:

> Mrs. Moore's and Adela's "passage to India" and Aziz's friendships, no less than the order of the Anglo-Indian community, rest on weak foundations. To a smaller or larger degree they are all based on a false assumption of order in the universe, and they do not recognize, or

42. Walter Allen, *The English Novel* (London: Phoenix House, 1954), p. 325.

43. Glen Pedersen, "Forster's Symbolic Form," *Kenyon Review* XXI (Spring 1959), 232.

44. See, for example, Doughty, "The Novels of E. M. Forster," pp. 542–49.

45. Wilde, *Art and Order: A Study of E. M. Forster*, p. 133.

cannot face, the disorder or chaos, even the variety, around them. All the meetings, all the attempts at communication are threatened by disruptive, disorderly, meaningless forces. Beneath all human efforts to give form to the world, to create civilization, lies, as the novel increasingly shows, nothing—no god, no first mover, no sustaining force.[46]

Many of the critics who consider Forster's message in *A Passage to India* to be totally pessimistic base their conclusions on what they take to be the novel's complete lack of union and unity. Samuel Hynes is one of these: "A more precise formulation of Forster's motto would be 'If only we *could* connect. . . . But, say the novels bleakly, we can't.'"[47] In line with this interpretation, Trilling writes: "The theme of separateness, of fences and barriers, the old theme of the Pauline epistles, which runs through all Forster's novels, is, in *A Passage to India*, hugely expanded and everywhere dominant. The separation of race from race, sex from sex, culture from culture, even of man from himself, is what underlies every relationship. The separation of the English from the Indians is merely the most dramatic of the chasms in this novel."[48] Alex Zwerdling is also concerned with the theme of separation in Forster's last novel: "This failure of intimacy between Fielding and Aziz is only the prime example of defeat in a book which is filled with partial and broken and unsatisfactory human relationships because of the disenchanted terms in which it views life." Zwerdling goes on to describe the atmosphere he finds in the novel as "a sense of weariness and fruitlessness, a world of isolation and solitude, in which people never quite come into each other's focus." He

46. Ibid., p. 130. It might be argued that Wilde, like Mrs. Moore, seems to have taken "the Marabar Caves as final."

47. Samuel Hynes, "The Old Man at King's," *Commonweal* LXXIX (February 21, 1964), 638.

48. Trilling, *E. M. Forster*, p. 151.

concludes that "there is little place for hope and expectation in such a world."[49]

There are readers who are not prepared to find the novel unreservedly affirmative but who balk at interpretations as bleak as those just quoted. These commentators occupy a middle ground between the more clear-cut positions of their colleagues. Some of them, like Gertrude M. White, judge the book to be almost as optimistic as do the critics in the affirmative camp: "It is the spirit of love, of intuitive understanding which triumphs at last, in spite of [Mrs. Moore's] personal defeat."[50] More typical of this group is the belief that, in the novel, Forster has defined a problem rather than answered it. Thus, Ellin Horowitz writes that Forster "has not chosen a way, but rather creates his novels out of antithesis, seeking resolution,"[51] and Reuben Brower asserts that there is no conclusion, just a belief in the possibility of human relations—relations which are always on the brink of a breakdown.[52]

In this discussion of the themes of *A Passage to India*, it should be pointed out that some critics' ideas do not fit any tidy schematization—George H. Thomson's notion that "the earth will not support man; man must give value to the earth," for example, or W. A. S. Keir's conviction that for Forster religion is the expression of, not the answer to, difficulties.[53] Nevertheless, two main areas of opinion—that the novel represents either a positive

49. Alex Zwerdling, "The Novels of E. M. Forster," *Twentieth Century Literature* II (January 1957), 181.

50. Gertrude M. White, "*A Passage to India*: Analysis and Revaluation," *PMLA* LXVIII (September 1953), 652.

51. Ellin Horowitz, "The Communal Ritual and the Dying God in E. M. Forster's *A Passage to India*," *Criticism* VI (Winter 1964), 70.

52. Brower, *The Fields of Light*, pp. 182–98.

53. George H. Thomson, "Thematic Symbol in *A Passage to India*," p. 53; W. A. S. Keir, "*A Passage to India* Reconsidered," *Cambridge Journal* V (April 1952), 431.

vision of love, order, and unity or a negative vision of despair, chaos, and separation—account for the great majority of critical responses.

There is a close connection, of course, between a critic's interpretation of the novel's theme and his explanation of its structure, of the symbolism of "Caves" and "Temple," and of the role played by reason and mysticism. Virtually every scholar has agreed that the major structure of *A Passage to India* is a triad, reflecting its triple division: "Mosque," "Caves," and "Temple."[54] In fact, the seeking of a complete set of parallels among the three sections has led to some ingenious readings.

The most widely agreed upon pattern in *A Passage to India* is the "rhythmic rise-fall-rise" that E. K. Brown first noted.[55] McConkey concurs that the novel possesses a rhythm of "rising, falling, and rising again which is also a return."[56] Several critics have elaborated this pattern most convincingly. V. A. Shahane finds in "Mosque" "an attempted getting together"; "Caves" "indicates frustration and alienation"; "Temple" signifies reconciliation "because the festival is symbolic of love and harmony." Shahane goes on to explicate the minor symbols in support of his thesis.[57] For Thomson, the book's first division is a "prelude, touching lightly on serious actions"; the second part illustrates a "physical and spiritual wasteland"; the last section reveals "the promise of spiritual achievement." Thomson correlates this sequence with "three stages of man's spiritual history or the individual's spiritual

54. It has been noted that Forster's second published novel, *The Longest Journey*, also uses a tripartite division—"Cambridge," "Sawston," and "Wiltshire"—which also lends itself to symbolic interpretations.

55. Brown, *Rhythm in the Novel*, p. 113.

56. McConkey, *The Novels of E. M. Forster*, p. 13.

57. V. A. Shahane, "Symbolism in E. M. Forster's *A Passage to India*: 'Temple,'" *English Studies* XLIV (December 1963), 424, 427.

development": a shallow stage, marked in the book by
Aziz's "superficial optimism," a stage of disillusionment,
embodied in Mrs. Moore's response to the Marabar, and
a stage of qualified achievement, exemplified by Godbole's
meditation at the Hindu festival. These stages, according
to Thomson, comprise the entire spiritual development of
Mrs. Moore.[58] Brown believes that these "three big
blocks of sound" disclose evil creeping about weakly
dominated by the secret understanding of the heart, evil
streaming forth from the caves but meeting opposition—
"indecisive in some ways"—from Godbole and Mrs.
Moore, and "evil forced to recede . . . by the strength on
which the secret understanding of the heart depends,
contemplative insight, intuitive fidelity. Then the final
reminder that good has merely obliged evil to recede as
good receded before evil a little before."[59] Also within the
province of this majority interpretation of the structure is
Brower's analysis: "Mosque" signifies the possibility of
communication between Englishmen and Indians—but
also its opposite; "Caves" parallels "Mosque," repeating
the same opposition of mystery and order, but intensifying
the disillusionment and muddle, the failure of communication; "Temple" emphasizes the possibility of revelation.[60]
Gertrude M. White, in her discussion of "Mosque,"
describes the series of "gaps" it uncovers—between Indian
and Briton, Moslem and Hindu, soldier and civilian,
major and minor official, man and woman, mankind and
creation. Two different types of unity are sought in
"Mosque": unity of negation, characterized by the
English hatred of Indians and its opposite, the unity of
affirmation, exemplified by the activities of Mrs. Moore
and Fielding. However, with the coming of the hot

58. Thomson, "Thematic Symbol in *A Passage to India*," p. 51.
59. Brown, *Rhythm in the Novel*, p. 113.
60. Brower, *The Fields of Light*, p. 184.

weather, the attempts of the latter two, and Aziz, meet with failure: the Caves symbolize "the rout of the forces of reconciliation, the complete triumph of hostility, evil, and negation. . . . The Marabar Caves are the very voice of that union which is the opposite of divine." Like the other commentators in this group, White thinks that "Temple" is an emblem of "reconciliation of differences not in negation but in a larger synthesis; of a universe which is perhaps a mystery rather than a muddle, a riddle to which an answer exists; and of the Rains, token of renewed life, of regeneration, and of hope."[61]

Aside from the large number of critics who share the prelude-separation-reconciliation interpretation of the novel's structural triad, there is a smaller group favoring a second explication: "Mosque," "Caves," and "Temple" symbolize emotion, reason, and love. Some of these commentators attempt to connect these three conditions with Islam, Anglo-India (or Christianity), and Hinduism; or with Aziz, Fielding (or Mrs. Moore), and Godbole. Such analysts do not seem troubled by the cross ranking of "emotion" and "love," but they do catch a glimmer of the difficulties presented by the equation of "Caves"-reason-Christianity-Mrs. Moore.

Glen O. Allen is one of the most stimulating proponents of the emotion-reason-love triad. He writes that Forster's basic categories are the "emotional nature, the intellect, and the capacity for love. [Forster] has accordingly selected religions to represent his views, each of which offers exercise predominantly to one of these faculties. . . . [The religion of caves is] devoted to reason, form, and the sense of purpose as the *sine qua non* of right behavior and attitude. . . . The principal function of the threefold division of the novel, then, is to represent these three

61. White, "*A Passage to India:* Analysis and Revaluation," pp. 644, 646, 647, 651.

'attitudes towards life' both as they partake of regularized religious views and as they are expressions of varying types of culture and of individual character."[62] In line with this schematization, Allen stresses Mrs. Moore's rationality rather than her mysticism: "Her strongest moorings are of ultimate intellectual origin . . . without being intellectually disposed, [she] is intellectually committed; without having the capacity for thought, she is nevertheless a victim of her intellectual heritage."[63] Wilfred Stone seems to both agree and disagree with Allen's explication: the three sections

> also stand for Moslem, Anglo-Indian, and Hindu, and for the qualities of character and temperament associated with these ethnic groups. Since Moslem-Mosque and Hindu-Temple clearly go together, it would seem logical to link Anglo-Indian and Caves—as Glen O. Allen has tried to do. . . . But actually the caves represent everything that the British, with their devotion to the daylight virtues of God, King, and Country, generally find incomprehensible or repugnant. If Forster had needed merely a parallel name, he could have called the middle section "The Club," which was Sawston-in-India's true church. But Mr. Allen is both perceptive and just in seeing that the three sections emphasize certain qualities of mind and soul—to the Moslem belongs the emotional nature, to the Anglo-Indian the intellect, and to the Hindu the capacity for love.[64]

This discussion is confusing. If the second section stands for Anglo-India, and if Anglo-India represents intellectualism, then how does "Caves" represent the opposite of intellectualism? And if Stone agrees with Allen about

62. Glen O. Allen, "Structure, Symbol, and Theme in *A Passage to India*," pp. 936, 937, 938.

63. Ibid., p. 937. But what is a thoughtless commitment if not an emotional attachment? Allen's categories overlap and intermix.

64. Stone, *The Cave and the Mountain*, p. 311.

the emphasis on British rationality in the second section, are they really in disagreement? Ironically, although both men are in accord, their harmony is based on their shared conviction that "Caves" really signifies an *attack* on British "devotion to reason, form, and the sense of purpose." Stone's position becomes clear in his extended Jungian analysis of the Marabar, but it turns out that Allen also finds in "Caves," not an expression of the religion of logic, but a manifestation of its antithesis: the reflection of the match in the cave wall points to the "inadequacy of intelligence or reason in its effort to discover within the limits of its categories the ultimate nature of the universe."[65] Thus, for these critics, the three sections seem to symbolize a positive view of the emotions, a negative appraisal of reason, an affirmative presentation of love—a scheme not as strictly parallel as the authors' quest for order might have led the reader to expect. Hugh Maclean also subscribes to the theory that "Caves" focuses on reason in order to show its inadequacies, but he contends, as well, that Forster's presentation of emotion as the motif of the first section is an attack, not an affirmation:

> the claims of emotion, logic, and intuition to be central in man's search for the meaning of life are critically examined in successive divisions of the book. . . . The opening segment of the novel, in short, is primarily negative and unsatisfactory. It prepares for late events. The way of Aziz, of emotion, sentiment, memory, is weak, and even reinforces the influence of self-centeredness in man and society. . . . Being British Fielding proceeds basically in terms of logic and intellect, and his thought gives the tone to [the second] section, as the emotions of Aziz coloured the first. . . . Emotion and logic are alike neglected [in the third section]; intuition

65. Glen O. Allen, "Structure, Symbol, and Theme in *A Passage to India*," p. 942.

has replaced them, and even that term is insufficiently descriptive of the mystical tone which pervades this section.[66]

With a few exceptions,[67] then, the critics of *A Passage to India* have interpreted "Mosque," "Caves," and "Temple" as representing either approach, separation, reunion; or emotion, intellect, love—depending, perhaps, on whether the author sees the novel in terms of movement or statement.

Just as the Marabar Caves engaged Forster's energy more than any other aspect of the novel,[68] they have most occupied the critics' attention. Termed by McConkey "the most provocative image of all Forster's novels"[69] the caves have been examined to ascertain if their meaning is related to Hinduism or some other metaphysical system, their echo has been pondered, their effects on Adela Quested and Mrs. Moore charted. Even Forster's rhetoric in regard to the caves has been analyzed; although this is one area where more work remains to be done, the best stylistic exegesis to date is offered in Frank Kermode's sensitive essay, "Mr. E. M. Forster As a Symbolist":

> One can start at the opening chapter, indeed the opening sentence. "Except for the Marabar Caves—and they are

66. Hugh Maclean, "The Structure of *A Passage to India*," *University of Toronto Quarterly* XXII (January 1953), 157, 163, 164, 168.

67. See, for example, Richard Kain's thesis that the three parts represent Muslim, Brahman, and Cosmic, respectively ("Vision and Discovery in E. M. Forster's *A Passage to India*," p. 263). Compare with this Karippacheril Chakko Eapen's theory that the three parts symbolize the Hindu trinity: "Mosque"-Brahman, "Caves"-Siva, "Temple"-Vishnu ("E. M. Forster and India" [Ph.D. diss., University of Colorado, 1962], p. 153). Keith Hollingsworth asserts that "Caves" embodies sciencism, the religion of the West ("*A Passage to India:* The Echoes in the Marabar Caves," *Criticism* IV [Summer 1962], 216).

68. See Chapter 3, p. 82.

69. McConkey, *The Novels of E. M. Forster*, p. 133.

twenty miles off—the city of Chandrapore presents nothing extraordinary." Easy, colloquial, if with a touch of the guide-book, the words set a scene. But they will reach out and shape the organic whole. Or, to put it another way, they lie there, lacking all rhetorical emphasis, waiting for the relations which will give them significance to the eye of "love." But they are prepared for these relations. The order of principal and subordinate clauses, for instance, is inverted, so that the exception may be mentioned first—"except for the Marabar Caves." The excepted is what must be included if there is to be meaning; first things first. First, then, the extraordinary which governs and limits significance; then, secondly, we may consider the city. It keeps the caves at a distance; it is free of mystery till nightfall, when the caves close in to question its fragile appearance of order—an appearance that depends upon a social conspiracy to ignore the extraordinary. Henceforth, in this novel, the word "extraordinary" is never used without reference to the opening sentence. It belongs to the caves. The last words of the first chapter speak once more of "the extraordinary caves." Miss Quested's behavior in relation to the caves is "extraordinary."[70]

Judged in the light of recent, complex interpretations, most of the earlier comments on the caves, such as David Cecil's, sound wonderfully clear and simple, probably too simple: "Some dangerous, hostile strain in the elemental constitution of things manifests itself in the caves, supernaturally, it would seem, affecting the characters."[71] Critics writing within the last decade have emphasized either the ambiguity or the inconclusiveness of the caves.

70. Frank Kermode, "Mr. E. M. Forster As a Symbolist," in *Forster: A Collection of Critical Essays*, p. 92. The essay first appeared in *The Listener*, January 2, 1958.

71. David Cecil, "E. M. Forster," *Atlantic Monthly* CLXXIII (January 1949), 61.

Thus, J. B. Beer writes, "Everything in the novel has to be confronted by the caves. The head of Adela and the heart of Mrs. Moore are equally challenged by the negation of a cave which can only reflect sights and sounds. For them it is a confrontation with 'reality' in the worst sense of the word: matter without mind, substance devoid of imaginative appeal. But this is not full reality even if it is an element without which reality cannot exist."[72]

Modern critics have attempted to use insights gained from the study of Hinduism or psychoanalysis—or, in the case of Wilfred Stone, of both—in order to facilitate their exploration of the Marabar. Stone, whose argument is difficult to paraphrase or condense, writes:

> The mountain and its hollow core, the body and its cavity, or even more generally, the circle within the circle, are archetypal picturings of life's origin, of the primal inside and outside from which creation springs. The Marabar Caves, antedating human religion and history, are "not holy" to the Hindu, yet what happened in that engendering egg is instinctively understood by Professor Godbole, the Hindu, while it only terrifies, puzzles, or bores the others. . . . The particular caves of the Marabar do not happen to be worshipped, but they have this universal symbolic meaning, a meaning that the Hindu preserves and venerates in the architecture of his temple. When Forster discovered the Hindu temple (years after *Passage* appeared), he did so with a delighted shock of recognition—as if the full meaning of his own book were only now opening to his expanding vision.
>
> Forster . . . was taught to see the temple as the "World Mountain," a mountain "on whose exterior is displayed life in all its forms, life human and superhuman and animal, life tragic and cheerful, cruel and kind, seemly and obscene, all crowded at the Mountain's

summit by the sun." In the interior of the mountain, he continues, there is "a tiny cavity, a central cell, where, in the heart of the world complexity, the individual could be alone with his god."[73]

I would like to interrupt Stone's interesting discussion to examine his major assumption—that, when Forster wrote *A Passage to India*, he knew more about the Indian temple than he realized he knew, until, sixteen years later, a "shock of recognition" revealed to him what he had meant in the novel. Forster's knowledge of Indian temples is crucial to the argument because Stone believes that the conception of the temple unlocks the significance of the caves and, in fact, of the whole novel. Stone is aware that Forster wrote in 1940, "I know some Hindu temples fairly well—for instance the great group at Khajraho in Bundelkand—but I have never understood what they were about; they were just a group of impressive buildings, very ornate outside, and rather poky inside. I grasped nothing further. Now I learn that...."[74] But he posits some sort of unconscious understanding of these matters on Forster's part. The only sound methodology for establishing Forster's alleged knowledge, it seems to me, is a careful reading to find expression of his conception in the novel. To hold that this knowledge is in the novel because, although Forster later learned it, he had really possessed it all along is to indulge in circular reasoning. To be sure, Stone analyzes the novel's section on the caves closely, but he does so largely on the basis of the assumption outlined above. Other critics have also used Forster's later writings about India to explicate the novel without giving any thought to this problem. What

73. Stone, *The Cave and the Mountain*, pp. 301–2. Ellin Horowitz, in "The Communal Ritual and the Dying God in E. M. Forster's *A Passage to India*," also asserts that "the Marabar Cave is both womb and grave" (p. 75).

74. E. M. Forster, "The Individual and His God," *Listener* XXIV (December 5, 1940), 801.

Stone has to say about the caves is, nevertheless, most absorbing and deserves to be quoted extensively:

> The caves, however, are not spiritually identical with the inner cell of the World Mountain; they are only its archetypal form. The architecture of the temple is a late and sophisticated shaping of a dim racial memory—of something primal, elemental, antecedent to consciousness. The caves hint at something existing before gods, before differentiation, before value. Though the temple remembers this form, and shapes itself around it as a shell around an egg, it is at a far remove from the caves' "unspeakable" nothingness. . . . The caves are the primal womb from which we all came and primal tomb to which we all return; they are the darkness before existence itself. Some can contemplate nothingness, others cannot. . . . The snake, too, is both beautiful and deadly: the shedding of its skin represents reincarnation or rebirth, and its circular coils represent the evolution of life. . . . Forster is particularly sensitive to the duality of consciousness and unconsciousness. The snakes in the stones of the Marabar Caves are reflections of the match flame—light brought in from a newer and relatively rational world outside—but they make visible other flames, other snakes, which we are to imagine as inhabiting the stone from the beginning, before man forced an entrance. . . . Consciousness and unconsciousness pursue each other in the novel, but they do not meet—and therein lies the world tragedy. . . . Thus in the novel the visitors to the caves are making a return from consciousness to unconsciousness, going back to a prehistoric and prerational condition from which they have been released, but which is still a lurking—though repressed—presence in them all.[75]

75. Stone, *The Cave and the Mountain*, pp. 304, 307, 308, 309–10. Stone's elaborate book is appliquéd with great swatches of Jungian psychoanalytic theory, Indian mythology, and archetypal analysis; in order to follow the line of the argument, the reader must thread his way painstakingly through all this dazzling stuff.

Glen O. Allen is also interested in the relation between the snake image and the cave that incorporates it. After attempting to prove that Atman and Brahman are in the cave, he quotes from the Vedanta-Sutras to the effect that the relationship between Atman (the transcendent self, the God dwelling within) and Brahman (the universal soul, the metaphysical absolute) is that of a snake to its coils. Allen continues, "The importance of the snake symbol, then, is the equivalent [*sic*] of the cave symbol itself—the ultimate identity of Brahman and Atman." Allen, like several other critics, connects the echo with the snake image that Forster uses to depict sound as it coils to the roof of the caves. The snake, which is also described in the novel as a serpent or worm, represents the "universal will" for Allen: "In the cave, the echo spoke out to her of the oneness of all things; it revealed itself to her as a serpent, the universal will, composed (under the principle of individuation) of a manifold of wills, writhing independently, struggling against each other."[76] Allen thus emphasizes in his entire discussion the symbolic unity the caves can offer rather than the cleavage between consciousness and unconsciousness that Stone finds so strong an element in the Marabar. McConkey finds both the separation between Atman and Brahman which consciousness fosters and a resolution, radical to Western thought, which he supposes the caves symbolize: the granite of the cave implies the "matter of the phenomenal universe; the reflection of the flame would be the Brahman that dwells in the stone, in all of the universe. But the phenomenal universe is but a mirror—the image holds not

76. Allen, "Structure, Symbol, and Theme in *A Passage to India*," pp. 942, 949. Stone, in *The Cave and the Mountain*, writes on this subject: "The echoes too—the aural equivalents of the 'snakes composed of small snakes, which writhe independently'—are made possible by that same air that feeds the flames, the air which carries waves of sound and through which light passes" (p. 310).

only in the passage, but elsewhere in the novel—and the
existence of the identical flame in the wall is actually
illusion. Union of Atman and Brahman can be achieved
only by the extinction of consciousness, by the expiration
of the match flame. It is once again the moment of
Nirvana (the word, in fact, refers to the 'blowing out' of
the flame of life), when the individual soul divorces itself
finally from consciousness and all illusion and merges with
the absolute." McConkey also takes up Allen's argument
that the echo-serpent represents the individual will, but
for McConkey it is individual consciousness, rather, that is
being evoked: "The echo, like the mirrored flame of which
it is the auditory equivalent, is the product of individual
consciousness: it is another sensory impression within the
illusory and finite world. Throughout the novel, it signifies
the return of sound from circular wall or arching sky,
sound reverberating in a world from which good is missing. To Adela, the echo in the cave has released evil."[77]

What did happen to Adela Quested in the Caves? Her
condition has been labeled psychologically: "something
like a mental blackout,"[78] and theologically: "defilement
of soul."[79] It has been attributed to her rationalism, by

77. McConkey, *The Novels of E. M. Forster*, pp. 147, 149. Keith Hollingsworth is another critic who equates the echo with the undying worm-snake
imagery. He tentatively puts forth the notion that the worm is death,
offering Biblical references in evidence ("*A Passage to India:* the Echoes in
the Marabar Caves," p. 212). In other commentaries on the echo, E. K.
Brown writes that it "removes distinctions" (*Rhythm in the Novel*, p. 98),
while Richard J. Voorhees holds that "the echo of the cave need not be
devastating because it is neutral"; the echo devastates those people who do
not understand or cannot accept its real meaning ("The Novels of E. M.
Forster," p. 97).

78. Maclean, "The Structure of *A Passage to India*," p. 165. "As a result
of her encounter with 'Boum,' she undergoes an actual split of soul from
body and from self" (p. 166).

79. Stanley Cooperman, "The Imperial Posture and the Shrine of
Darkness: Kipling's *The Naulahka* and E. M. Forster's *A Passage to India*,"
English Literature in Transition VI, no. 1 (1963), 10.

Allen: "Adela's wish for explanation at all cost is the source of her error"[80]—a rationalism which some critics consider responsible for her rejection of "unconscious feeling" and her continued existence in a world of illusion and fragmentation.[81] Louise Dauner, presenting this view, believes that in the cave Adela confronts the "male principle" that woman carries within her—Jung's "animus"—which the girl rejects as evil.[82] Stone finds Miss Dauner's interpretation perceptive, but modifies it because an encounter with "animus" would not sufficiently account for Adela's terror. He believes Adela experiences "shadow," the bottom of the unconscious, which horrifies those unequipped for the meeting. Attempting to explain "shadow" further, Stone quotes from Jung's *The Archetypes and the Collective Unconscious* as follows:

> The meeting with oneself is, at first, the meeting with one's own shadow. The shadow is a tight passage, a narrow door, whose painful constriction no one is spared who goes down to the deep well. But one must learn to know oneself in order to know who one is. For what comes after the door is, surprisingly enough, a boundless expanse full of unprecedented uncertainty, with apparently no inside and no outside, no above and no below, no here and no there, no mine and no thine, no good and no bad. It is the world of water, where all life floats in suspension; where the realm of the sympathetic system, the soul of everything living, begins; where I am indivisibly this *and* that; where I experience the other in myself and the other-than-myself experiences me.[83]

80. Glen O. Allen, "Structure, Symbol, and Theme in *A Passage to India*," p. 940.

81. Louise Dauner, "What Happened in the Cave? Reflections on *A Passage to India*," *Modern Fiction Studies* VII (Autumn 1961), 262. The term *unconscious feeling* is confusing since most people understand the word *feeling* as implying "awareness."

82. Ibid.

83. Stone, *The Cave and the Mountain*, p. 335.

Adela feels "shadow," Stone continues, "as a kind of rape of the personality" because the experience of meeting herself as something other has been "unbearably abnormal." But Adela somehow senses her irresponsibility in refusing to assimilate her unconscious and feels guilty, accordingly.[84] This complex analysis may throw light on much of Adela's behavior. Another account of her situation, one which makes Stone's seem unadventurous by comparison, was offered in the *New Statesman* two months after the novel was first published. It is E. A. Horne's contention that Aziz suffered the delusion of rape and communicated it to Adela. Horne describes this as "rich material for a psychoanalyst," but it seems a more appropriate concern for a medium. In support of his position, the author offers Aziz's sexual vanity and physical "obsessions," and Adela's "impressionable mind," as evidenced by her susceptibility to Mrs. Moore's preoccupation with "evil spirits."[85]

Unlike Adela's experience in the cave, Mrs. Moore's visit has little effect on the plot of *A Passage to India*, but critics have been even more concerned with what happened to Mrs. Moore in the Marabar—and with her general significance in the novel—than with the difficulties of her younger companion. The problem of understanding Mrs. Moore's ambiguous character and experience may be attributed to Forster's great subtlety, but it may also be owing, in part, to his changing conception of her as he worked on the book.[86] In either event, few commentators have been willing to take a clear-cut stand, whether to label her a "Magna Mater"[87] and "fertility

84. Ibid., p. 336.
85. E. A. Horne, "Mr. Forster's *A Passage to India*," p. 543.
86. See Chapter 3, pp. 105–107.
87. Walter Allen, *The English Novel*, p. 325. See also Warner, *E. M. Forster*: "From the outlook of liberal rationalism it may seem impossible to justify this strange figure—a wise woman without any evident wisdom, a

goddess"[88] or an earth mother whose "milk is soured and
. . . womb diseased,"[89] without wanting to qualify their
assessments. Mrs. Moore has several supporters. Some stress
the sensitivity that lets her come "closest to understanding
India because she adopts the Hindu view of life,"[90] or
admire "the intuitive insight of Mrs. Moore, who feels the
presence of God in the mosque and awakens an immediate
response from Dr. Aziz";[91] others praise her unifying
power: "Mrs. Moore is symbolic of the external influence
which can metamorphose lesser nature, and through her
the essential characters involved in their various ways of
life are united in the eternal, baptismal waters."[92] But
most critics tend to reflect Mrs. Moore's ambivalence in
their own writings. Brown, for example, believes that
Forster's values are "better apprehended by Mrs. Moore"
than by Fielding, even though the old lady quotes St.
Paul who, as Brown remembers, is not Forster's lawgiver,
and even though she is irritable and of uncertain sympathies: "The artist's imaginative sympathies [have

---

Christian lapsed into emptiness, a kind of Magna Mater the echo of whose
drum is not ecstatic, though she seems to exact from her worshippers a
willing or reluctant emasculation. . . . It may be said that Mrs. Moore is a
link between Christianity and the atmosphere of barely understood
Hinduism with which the book ends" (pp. 26–27).

88. Horowitz, "The Communal Ritual and the Dying God in E. M.
Forster's *A Passage to India*," p. 75.

89. Doughty, "The Novels of E. M. Forster," p. 549.

90. Oliver, *The Art of E. M. Forster*, p. 72.

91. Kain, "Vision and Discovery in E. M. Forster's *A Passage to India*,"
p. 262. He also praises Mrs. Moore for her healing powers: "And though she
closed her life with an almost petulant indifference, it was her spirit that
healed the wounds of misunderstanding between Aziz and Fielding" (p. 172).

92. Pedersen, "Forster's Symbolic Form," p. 241. Pedersen also holds
that "Mrs. Moore's immortality comes from the form inherent in her
character. All the other characters realize form in their individual degrees
relative to her. And community living is fulfilled only to the extent that
others realize her depth in space and her transcendence in time. But her
fourth dimension remained a mystery" (p. 239).

ɔutrun] his intellectual commitments."[93] And Hugh
Maclean thinks that her experience in the Marabar
ɔannot be totally negative since something good grows
ɔut of it: "What happens to Mrs. Moore in the cave is not
ɔo much evil in itself as it is a necessary preparation for the
ɔonsequent freeing of good influences to act in a way
previously impossible."[94]

There is a group of critics who are skeptical of the idea
that Forster intended any aura of sanctification to sur-
round Mrs. Moore or any intimation that her vision in the
cave is an enlightening one in which she glimpses cosmic
unity. Thus, Brower believes that Mrs. Moore cannot
become in tune with the infinite because of the "mocking
denial of her echo": neither Mrs. Moore nor her children
experience oneness with the universe.[95] Edwin Nierenberg
notes that even before the trip to the Marabar, Mrs.
Moore's religion is incomplete because "she has an
innocent conception of evil, and because her piety is
unfulfilled by *acts* of love." Although concerned with duty,
she fosters a marriage that she knows is not based on love.
Dwelling on rewards in the hereafter, Mrs. Moore can no
longer do her duty when, after the expedition to the caves,
she loses belief in the possibility of being rewarded: "She
cannot sing to a God who will never come." Nierenberg
considers as symptomatic of Mrs. Moore's failings her
inability, when she views the Ganges with Ronny and

93. Brown, *Rhythm in the Novel*, p. 144. He finds Mrs. Moore, like Ruth
Wilcox of *Howards End*, "a redemptive character; unable to save herself, she
did miraculous things for others. . . . The beneficent influence of Mrs.
Moore flows out of the secret understanding of the heart" (p. 109). Lionel
Trilling, in *E. M. Forster*, expresses a similar view: Mrs. Moore "has had the
beginning of the Hindu vision of things and it has crushed her." But her
influence is pervasive and benevolent. "Despite the sullen disillusionment in
which Mrs. Moore died, she had been right when she had said to Ronny
that there are many kinds of failure, some of which succeed" (pp. 158, 159).
94. Maclean, "The Structure of *A Passage to India*," p. 157.
95. Brower, *The Fields of Light*, p. 184.

Adela, to accept *both* the beauty of the river and its terror.
In sum, Mrs. Moore "fails because she is not wise enough
in her good will to accept muddle or mystery in' a friend,
a God or India."[96] Nierenberg expresses more doubts
about Mrs. Moore's claims to wisdom than does any other
critic with the exception of Frederick C. Crews, who
considers at length Mrs. Moore's failure of understanding
and the ironic benevolence of her influence. He asks why
Mrs. Moore,

> who seems to have a second sight on occasion and who
> is certainly a morally sympathetic character, is visited
> with disillusionment. One answer may simply be that she
> *does* have second sight, that she perceives what truly
> subsists behind the veil of Maya; in this case her ex-
> perience would constitute a thorough disavowal of
> Hinduism on Forster's part. Remembering Adela's
> hallucination, however, we may question whether Mrs.
> Moore has penetrated anything at all. Perhaps she has
> merely heard echoes of her own unvoiced misgivings
> about the significance of life.

In any case, says Crews, the popular reading that Mrs.
Moore "has experienced the merging of Atman and
Brahman" cannot be supported, for she is

> unprepared to relinquish her selfhood in the narrow
> sense of personality. Instead of blending her identity
> with that of the world-soul, she reduces the world-soul
> to the scale of her own wearied ego; her dilettantish
> yearning for oneness with the universe has been echoed,
> not answered. . . . She does not stay to testify for Aziz,
> for the moral issue of the trial cannot interest her; if there
> is no value in the universe, there is surely none in dis-
> tinctions between sanctioned and illicit love. Yet this

96. Edwin Nierenberg, "The Withered Priestess: Mrs. Moore's Incomplete Passage to India," *Modern Language Quarterly* XXV (June 1964), pp.
199, 200, 201.

very indifference makes it proper that Mrs. Moore, after she has withered out of bodily existence, should be resurrected as a Hindu goddess in the minds of the Indians at Aziz's trial. "When all the ties of the heart are severed here on earth," says the *Katha-Upanished*, "then the mortal becomes immortal." The parallel is in one sense ironic, as we have seen: Mrs. Moore has been the victim of a travesty of Hindu enlightenment. On the other hand, the Mrs. Moore who originally be-friended Aziz and who is remembered fondly by Professor Godbole has believed in loving everything that enters her consciousness, and such a love is the corner-stone of Hinduism.[97]

Mrs. Moore's negative vision in the cave is further elaborated by Gertrude M. White who asserts that unity becomes, for the old lady, "an infinity of Nothing. Good and evil are identical." Agreeing with Crews, Mrs. White writes, "To the Christian mystic the Marabar had said that the universe is muddle rather than mystery, the answer to its riddle is Nothingness."[98]

Some commentators, among these Karippacheril Chakko Eapen, take the view that, even if she is not spiritually developed enough to interpret the meaning of the caves soundly, Mrs. Moore has, at least, set her foot on the path of enlightenment. He believes that Mrs. Moore, because she possesses intuitive power, a spiritual affinity with Hinduism, and a desire to achieve oneness with the universe, is granted a vision of the Nadanta Dance—the dance of cosmic activity—by Siva, the God who is the third aspect of the Hindu triad and who Eapen believes is "the deity of the Marabar." Siva denies Mrs. Moore *moksa*, or liberation: although she understands his dance, she has not reached the stage of spiritual perfection required for salvation. She does become an ascetic and a

97. Crews, *The Perils of Humanism*, pp. 158–59, 160–61.
98. White, "*A Passage to India:* Analysis and Revaluation," p. 648.

devotee of Siva.[99] Another interpretation, not totally
bleak, is developed by Alan Wilde: Mrs. Moore's
experience in the Marabar is not final for her. (Few
critics have ever thought that the caves are final for
Forster.) He holds that her despair after the journey to the
Marabar does not prevent Mrs. Moore from communica-
ting subverbally to Adela her regard for Aziz and that,
on the journey home, she concludes the message of the
caves to be not nihilism but stoicism:

> In the fact of so many and so diverse customs, cultures,
> and religions, the old woman is unable to retain her
> belief in an ordered world overseen by the Christian
> God; confronted by Mohammedanism, by Hinduism,
> by an India so different from the tidier England she has
> known, she succumbs, fully now, to the blight of relativ-
> ism. Her cosmos is shattered and she withdraws into
> all that is left her as solid and substantial—into herself.
> Her desire to communicate disappears, and she sinks
> into a profound state of cynical indifference, able only
> barely to keep herself from complete engulfment. . . .

For Wilde, Mrs. Moore's bitterness hinders verbal communication: yet she manages to convey to Adela that
Aziz is innocent. Wilde believes that

> On some deeper level, her more fundamental interest
> in people and her desire to love them and see them happy
> assert themselves and make themselves known in
> mysterious ways. Her regard for Aziz penetrates through
> her indifference and her blasphemy, since, in con-
> firming Adela's own doubts about the incident, she is
> preparing for his ultimate vindication. The knowledge

99. Eapen, "E. M. Forster and India," p. 146. Eapen offers much the
same evidence to sustain his theory that Siva, the destroyer, is the God of the
Marabar, but since the snake, tiger, bull, and elephant—as well, undoubt-
edly, as other animals—are all connected with him, along with the moon,
flame, the color blue, and many other objects and attributes, finding Siva
symbols in "Caves" becomes a game with virtually no rules.

must be communicated without words, from some depth
unaffected by the shattering of her world picture, but it
is communicated. . . . [During the journey home] the
world changes from the phantasmagoric reflection of her
own sense of flux into a more stable world of objects.
Life seems to her indestructible, though changing, and
asserts its independence of her particular view of it. Her
bitterness begins to decrease. . . . She learns that what
she saw in the caves was true, but that it was not all. . . .
Mrs. Moore was, in fact, not wrong in what she saw, but
wrong in the way she saw it, wrong not in assuming that
beneath all man's efforts there lies an abyss, but in
refusing to go on despite (but not ignoring) the fact.[100]

But the debate about whether Mrs. Moore understands
the message of the caves correctly—and, if she does,
whether she accepts it or rejects it—has many partici-
pants. Kermode and Allen are in approximate accord that
Mrs. Moore's vision is genuine and that in embracing it
she loses the possibility of happiness. McConkey thinks
that Mrs. Moore's understanding is incomplete and that
it is this partial comprehension that leads to her despair.
Kermode writes: "Mrs. Moore accepts [the caves], seeing
a whole, but one in which love is absent; all distinctions
obliterated not by meaning but by meaninglessness, the
roar of the Marabar echo. Including the excepted does not
necessarily result in felicity."[101] Glen O. Allen's version
agrees: "She was not able to explain that meaning [of the
caves] to Adela any more than Professor Godbole could
describe the caves for Aziz, for the meaning of such an
experience transcends the principle of individuation and
hence defies all attempts to conceptualize it. . . . But
Godbole had suggested to her what she was to find confirmed in her experience in the caves—that the costs of
being 'one with the universe' are the loss of a transcendent

100. Wilde, *Art and Order: A Study of E. M. Forster*, pp. 139, 142, 143, 144.
101. Kermode, "Mr. E. M. Forster As a Symbolist," p. 93.

sanction for values, the loss of absolute distinctions between good and evil, the loss of that ultimate reward for good works which made her accept duties as bearable, and, finally, the loss of that sublime emotion which comes from contemplating God in the infinitudes."[102] That Mrs. Moore's partial vision is actually an inadequate response to the meaning of the caves is the burden of McConkey's argument:

> [The Marabar] has caused Mrs. Moore to become aware, if but inadequately, of a transcendent principle which goes far beyond the divine reality which she has always perceived—so far beyond, in fact, that her whole scheme of values based upon that divine reality is demolished. . . . It is Siva, certainly, who emerges triumphant after Mrs. Moore's vision in the cave; a sense of evil, an absence of good, is the dominant note throughout most of the central section of the novel.
>
> Yet it is appropriate here to recall Forster's suggestion that "apathy, uninventiveness, and inertia" may be required before man can achieve "a sprouting of new growth through the decay"; Mrs. Moore's negating vision is a requisite for any new spiritual growth in a society that has lost contact with earth. . . . What must be stressed is that Mrs. Moore's love cannot exist in a world from which good is absent: the presence of good is evidence to her of God's existence.

What then is the truth of the Marabar that Mrs. Moore misses? McConkey answers:

> The central symbol of the Marabar Caves, which has so often perplexed the reader of Forster, becomes more explicable, though still no less the mystery it is intended to be, when the reader perceives the emptiness of the caves to be, on one level, a representation of the absolute Brahman in Hindu philosophy—empty, devoid of

102. Glen O. Allen, "Structure, Symbol, and Theme in *A Passage to India*," p. 949.

attributes, the ultimate reality beyond time and space and hence beyond human comprehension, with which the individual soul will finally merge.[103]

Still another question to be considered in penetrating the world of *A Passage to India* is the significance of the novel's last section, "Temple"—especially the views about Hinduism and Professor Godbole that it expresses. As has been indicated in the discussion of the structure of the book, most critics find the tone of "Temple" to be affirmative and its presentation of Hindus sympathetic: Parry writes that "their religion is for them a living force, embracing as it does all spirit and all matter and inter-twining the secular with the divine."[104] Some critics note that a gap is shown to exist between the "ideal of universal salvation" and the "attainment" of Godbole, who is, nevertheless, according to Thomson, "spiritually the most highly developed character in the novel."[105] But despite

103. McConkey, *The Novels of E. M. Forster*, pp. 136, 140, 144, 152. It will be noted that McConkey, like Eapen, subscribes to the theory that Siva is the spirit who pervades the Marabar. But for McConkey, Siva is a harbinger of the evil that results from the expedition. The discussion of the sacred *OM* probably owes much to Glen O. Allen who appears to have been the scholar to introduce the idea that *OM*, "the three-fold mani-festation of Godhead," is really the sound of the caves ("Structure, Symbol, and Theme in *A Passage to India*," p. 942). Aside from there being no evidence that Forster was familiar with this concept, the commonsensical reservation crops up, that between *OM*, however pronounced, and the echo's "boum" or "ou-boum"—transcribed in the *MS* "bou-oum" and "bou-ou-oum" (R. L. Harrison, "The Manuscript of *A Passage to India*" [Ph.D. diss., University of Texas, 1964], p. 292), Allen's "there is little phonetic dif-ference" is really questionable. Despite most critics' eagerness to embrace a metaphysical *origin* of the echo, I think Forster's variant orthography shows he may have been trying to create the actual sound of an echo that im-pressed him on a visit to Indian caves.

104. Benita Parry, "Passage to More Than India," p. 164.

105. Thomson, "Thematic Symbol in *A Passage to India*," p. 61. Thomson finds the tone of "Temple" a combination of the "serious and ironically urbane." He thinks that the festival at Mau is not an expression of organized religion, but of the religious spirit in action—not exclusive, but inclusive (pp. 61, 56).

this reservation, most commentators believe that Godbole is the character whom Forster regards as coming closest to the truth. Yet curiously, the general opinion is that, although Forster admires Godbole, he does not endorse Hinduism as the answer for all men.

Godbole is frequently compared with Mrs. Moore, almost always to the detriment of the old lady. Brown writes that they are "mysteriously alike"—both are attracted, for example, by "the trivial wasp"—but Mrs. Moore "has not come so far as he along the mystical path."[106] Parry sees the difference between them as much greater: "In her moment of anti-vision Mrs. Moore, nurtured in concepts of exclusive truths ('God is Love'), understands the message of the Caves and of India to be: 'Everything exists, nothing has value.' Hinduism has nothing in common with this nihilism, and the novel moves away from it. Godbole distinguishes between good and evil and defines their nature, and his concepts are played back through the thoughts and reactions of the other characters."[107] Kermode is in substantial agreement with Miss Parry, but he emphasizes Godbole's ability to understand that absence is not the same thing as non-existence: "Godbole can distinguish between presence and absence, and it is Mrs. Moore who cannot, and who therefore becomes a saint of Nothingness."[108] While concurring that Godbole is more advanced spiritually than is Mrs. Moore, McConkey feels that the major difference between them is that Godbole does not require a mani-

106. Brown, *Rhythm in the Novel*, p. 95.

107. Parry, "Passage to More Than India," p. 165. Keir holds the same opinion: Godbole in his disquisition on good and evil sees their difference as well as their relation. After the caves, Mrs. Moore sees good and evil as the same ("*A Passage to India* Reconsidered," p. 431).

108. Kermode, "Mr. E. M. Forster as a Symbolist," p. 95. On the same point, Thomson writes: Mrs. Moore has awareness of the absence of God, Godbole of his presence ("Thematic Symbol in *A Passage to India*," p. 59).

festation of benevolence on the human plane in order to maintain his faith: "Godbole, unlike Mrs. Moore, requires no belief that God can come to him; unlike Mrs. Moore, he does not even need to sense the principle of good in the world about him." It is McConkey's contention that "Godbole is the only person in all the novels who becomes the character-equivalent of the Forsterian voice." One of this critic's most important concepts, the "Forsterian voice" he defines as "a major aspect of the author's own vision . . . possessing as it does the compassion combined with the remove, the detachment, which one normally associates with the Christian saint or the devout Brahman." Thus, McConkey finds that Godbole's "position is one of detachment from human reality and from the physical world, a detachment gained by as complete a denial of individual consciousness as is possible, that denial and remove bringing with them a sense of love and an awareness of unity. For him, as for the Forsterian voice, a full perception of the transcendent reality is impossible, as is a full awareness of the unity within the physical world; but his achievement, though partial, though won only by renunciation, is still a victory, and the only victory that mankind, divorced from a friendly earth, can achieve!"[109] Gertrude M. White goes as far as McConkey in stressing that the Professor symbolizes the novel's moral core: "Godbole, then, stands for the union in reality of all men, whether they will or no, and for a universe in which God exists, though he may at a particular time and place not be present for a universe which may be a mystery but is not a muddle."[110]

Amid these voices of almost universal accord, one naysayer raises a protest: David Shusterman, single-handedly, mans a frontal assault against Godbole. The Professor is

109. McConkey, *The Novels of E. M. Forster*, pp. 142, 11, 5, 11–12.
110. White, "*A Passage to India*: Analysis and Revaluation," p. 652.

not a force of the good, but rather one who is evil or at least tends toward evil. Shusterman sees Fielding as the "sensitive, considerate, plucky aristocrat . . . who aspires to complete individual development and to a love with such another one as himself. . . . There is no equivalence between his love and Godbole's." Godbole should have told the visitors what they would find in the Marabar— although I am not sure how Shusterman wants him to explain the caves, even should he be able to anticipate the responses of each member of the party. In any event, Godbole's "attitude and behavior" make for "disharmony"; he is a "disruptive force," the "instigator of the wrongs . . . that result from the misunderstanding about the true nature of the Marabar." Westerners encounter in him an "impenetrable confusion" which stems, in turn, from his "bafflement because his implorings for the clarity of religious and cosmic knowledge have been met with silence by his God." He is, of course, not really tranquil; nor has he "an iota of warmth."[111]

As I have already stated, not many critics think that Forster is advocating Hinduism as the answer to the problems of Western man, even when the writers are convinced of Forster's approval of Godbole. A few—J. K. Johnstone, Thomson, McConkey—emphasize the strengths Forster has granted the Hindu position, but the majority offer qualified appraisals of Forster's final attitude. Johnstone believes that Forster is more sympathetic to Hinduism than to Islam or Christianity because they exclude too much, particularly evil; they are helpless

111. David Shusterman, "The Curious Case of Professor Godbole: *A Passage to India* Reexamined," *PMLA* LXXVI (September 1961), 427, 429, 430, 434. Shusterman raises some interesting points that the critical consensus had ignored: why, for example, didn't Godbole tell Aziz that Fielding had married Stella, not Adela? But he characteristically overstates the case, as in this instance, when he decides that Godbole, who asks Aziz to forgive his limitations, is really no friend of his at all.

before the caves.[112] Johnstone's positive argument in favor of the Hindu view is certainly not very strong when compared with Thomson's interpretation of the scene on the tank: "God is the unattainable ideal; he is the universe; he is the spirit of all men united in love and informing all matter with life. As actuality he is inconceivable; but unattainable, he can be apprehended. He is the goal (universal oneness), the spiritual reality (love) toward which man aspires."[113] This commitment, Thomson indicates, is Hinduism's and Forster's. McConkey also analyzes the Gokul Ashtami festival in order to understand its metaphysical significance. He suggests that, while the novelist's desires are those of the Hindu mystic, Forster may be pessimistic about man's willingness to submit to such a vision:

> Basic to the Mau ceremonies and to Godbole's desire "to attempt the stone" are the dual realities of Hindu metaphysics. Brahman is the unseen metaphysical absolute; the triad of Vishnu, Siva, and Brahma is the manifestation of Brahman. . . . The triad, indeed, as is true of the phenomenal universe itself, offers a reality which is but illusory; hence identification with the absolute comes only with the extinction of individual consciousness, with the final and total separation of soul from the physical realm. . . . The detachment and self-abnegation of Godbole are qualities which impart to him his extensive, though necessarily incomplete, sense of love and unity— even as they have always been the qualities of the Forsterian voice, imparting much the same incomplete vision.
>
> And so the rebirth suggested in the final pages of the novel is one to be brought about by a love which, in turn, can be obtained only through as great a denial of

112. J. K. Johnstone, *The Bloomsbury Group* (New York: Noonday Press, 1963), p. 261.
113. Thomson, "Thematic Symbol in *A Passage to India*," p. 62.

self and the physical world as it is possible for mankind to make. Is such a price too dear? Does the cost of love make the love prohibitive?[114]

The very transcendence and detachment of Hinduism that McConkey finds essential elements of its plan of salvation are attacked by Pedersen, who finds that Godbole exemplifies harmony, but that Godbole's way has "no community effect": "The Temple, India's most powerful effect, is nevertheless not dynamic enough to effect India's salvation. Essentially its lack of effect lies in detachment, a too strong desire for transcendence. The Hindus' aversion to the unwashed will continually preclude their coming to a desire for baptism for others. Only through an external influence will the unwashed become washed. When the Indians wash the calisthenic 'punkah wallah,' this strong, natural form will become *completely* beautiful, but the temple has not that in it which will effect the metamorphosis."[115] Allen is in agreement with McConkey that salvation is achieved through "denial of self," but he finds such denial tantamount to death and is relieved that Forster does not, in his opinion, suggest it: "Passage is the mystical return which can occur only with the complete renunciation of the will and utter loss of individuality in union with the whole. Such renunciation and loss [are] the equivalent of death. Forster does not propose this unhappy extreme."[116] Ellin Horowitz assents: The time is not yet for the Hindu mysticism which rejects both form and will.[117] Other critics express, in a variety of ways, their doubts that Forster is espousing Hinduism. White holds that Forster

114. McConkey, *The Novels of E. M. Forster*, pp. 87–88.

115. Pedersen, "Forster's Symbolic Form," pp. 239, 241.

116. Glen O. Allen, "Structure, Symbol, and Theme in *A Passage to India*," p. 953.

117. Horowitz, "The Communal Ritual and the Dying God in E. M. Forster's *A Passage to India*," p. 86.

espouses love in the novel, but she does not limit the way of love to Hinduism.[118] Keir believes that Forster holds himself aloof from Godbole's vision as well as Mrs. Moore's because, although India calls "Come," she is only an appeal not a promise.[119] And Wilde suggests that Forster may reject Hinduism for the values of the Mediterranean world. He finds it difficult to decide were in *A Passage to India* Forster's sympathies lie, but is certain that when Forster describes Venice there is "an enthusiasm and a straightforward affirmation" not found elsewhere in the book. "It is important, therefore," Wilde writes, "to remember Fielding's reaction to Venice, and not to simplify Forster's view of life into merely an affirmation of subrational communication: form, harmony, and reason receive, this once at least, their tribute as well."[120]

Even those critics who hesitate to label Forster's views in *A Passage to India* "mystical" concur in maintaining that the novel presents a gloomy appraisal of the ability of rationalism to solve mankind's dilemmas. The most that David Shusterman can claim is that nowhere in his writings does Forster "advocate complete detachment from human reality and from the physical world."[121] Most commentators go further. Ted Boyle calls the theme of the novel "the failure of untempered rationalism to destroy the barriers which isolate man from his fellow."[122] That Fielding is a man of good will is agreed upon, but so is the judgment that his good will is not enough. Brown writes: "Even though Fielding is tolerant, good tempered, and sympathetic, *A Passage to India* is not conceived

118. White, "*A Passage to India:* Analysis and Revaluation," p. 655.

119. Keir, "*A Passage to India* Reconsidered," p. 431.

120. Wilde, *Art and Order: A Study of E. M. Forster*, p. 149.

121. Shusterman, "The Curious Case of Professor Godbole: *A Passage to India* Reexamined," p. 426.

122. Ted E. Boyle, "Adela Quested's Delusion: The Failure of Rationalism in *A Passage to India*," *College English* XXVI (March 1965).

according to Fielding's liberal, skeptical, human values."[123] This opinion coincides with McConkey's appraisal of the limits of reason:

> Fielding and Godbole, those entirely different men, represent the division that exists between seen and unseen worlds; and they represent as well the disparity to be found between Forster's commitment to human relations and his commitment to the insight and love gained through a remove from those relations. . . . Fielding, despite his efforts in behalf of Aziz, still is denied brotherhood with him; thus, those efforts, admirable though they may be, can produce no lessening of the spiritual sterility. . . . Fielding's clarity of reason, his desire to achieve brotherhood among men, his acceptance of the physical world as "reality": these are not only desirable qualities, but necessary ones. Yet in a world of spiritual disintegration, a world upon whose surface man is a stranger, a wanderer without a home, the qualities of a Fielding will bring no new integration: they make the earth no less hostile, they impart no sense of connection between man and that which is more than man.[124]

Forster is never accused of being anti-intellectual, of course; his own reasonableness and humanistic bent are too widely acknowledged. Rather, he is seen as a man who, through devotion to reason, has come to understand how circumscribed is the province it governs, and who hopes, not to abandon it, but to augment it with some instinctive, intuitive, suprarational adjunct which will open up a new vista.

Interest in Forster as a symbolist is widespread. If the variety and ingenuity of the interpretations are any indication, he must be rated an accomplished practitioner.

123. Brown, *Rhythm in the Novel*, p. 114.
124. McConkey, *The Novels of E. M. Forster*, pp. 88–89, 159.

Despite the analysis of a large number of his symbols, no study has yet appeared devoted to his method. A minuscule anthology of Forster's devices—from title to wasp to tank—as explicated by his critics will reveal the range of their interest.

Many of the novel's interpreters have pointed out that its title, taken from Walt Whitman's poem of the same name, attaches much of the meaning of Whitman's poem to itself. Oliver believes the title is appropriate: "Whitman, celebrating further triumphs of civilization in the opening of the Suez Canal and the spanning of America by rail, writes of the need to combine with these material successes of Western civilization a new passage or voyage of the soul into those unexplained areas which are to the soul what India was to an early explorer like Vasco de Gama."[125]

The stone which appears at the novel's climax when Professor Godbole attempts to "impel" it during his religious ecstasy to "that place where completeness can be found" is explained by J. B. Beer as representing all that is inexorably unyielding in the universe: "There is always something that resists and denies love, and the stone is reminiscent of the intractable Marabar caves. Forster's inclusion of this intractable element even in Godbole's ecstatic dance is another indication of its importance in the novel as a whole. Once again, he insists on having a Caliban on his island."[126]

Illuminations of some of the novel's small emblems have been offered by various critics. Pedersen thinks that Mrs. Moore's game of patience is symbolic of the patience she

125. Oliver, *The Art of E. M. Forster*, p. 57. It should be noted that in the MS of the novel, Forster uses the title—which he does not do in the published work. After "the God to be thrown was an emblem of that" (p. 315), Forster had originally written: "Why this sacrifice at the heart of creation? To ask this question is to be sensible, but none who asks it will make passage to India" (Harrison, "The Manuscript," p. 699).

126. Beer, *The Achievement of E. M. Forster*, p. 160.

must exercise while others fail to see her way, "the way of inner revelation";[127] Nierenberg, however, likens Mrs. Moore's life to the patience pack, diminished by the meaningless cycle.[128] He also analyzes the meaning of the Tank of the Dagger, the pool at the Marabar Caves that Godbole discusses with Fielding. He believes that the legend, which describes the expiation of evil through the office of charity, illustrates "a moral complexity in which evil and good are mysteriously mixed."[129] Another metaphor of Indian lore, the Shrines of the Head and the Body which figure in the final section, are discussed by Allen. He thinks that the two shrines, which were necessitated by a young martyr's refusal to die when he was beheaded and who went on, instead, to collapse at his mother's house, symbolize the "awkward dichotomy" that "plans of salvation by religion" have left us.[130]

One of the most satisfactory explications in Forster criticism is E. K. Brown's discussion of the wasp and the bees. The following extracts will suggest the quality of close and sensitive reading in this model analysis:

> None of the sundried Anglo-Indians would have called the wasp a pretty dear; all of them would have been irritated by the wasp's inability to discriminate a house from a tree, which is India's inability, India's disinclination, to make the sharp tidy distinctions by which the Western intelligence operates. . . . The disturbing noises which accompany Mrs. Moore's gesture of affection and consideration—the minatory baying of the jackals and

127. Pederson, "Forster's Symbolic Form," p. 236.

128. Nierenberg, "The Withered Priestess: Mrs. Moore's Incomplete Passage to India," p. 202. Paul Fussel, Jr., in "E. M. Forster's Mrs. Moore: Some Suggestions," *Philological Quarterly* XXXII (October 1953), p. 389, uses Mrs. Moore's fondness for patience as one of her similarities to Madame Blavatsky, on whose character he thinks Mrs. Moore was partly based.

129. Nierenberg, "The Withered Priestess," p. 202.

130. Glen O. Allen, "Structure, Symbol and Theme in *A Passage to India*," p. 951.

percussion of drums—offer an undertone of suggestion that, unexpectedly beautiful and adequate as Mrs. Moore's response to Aziz and to the wasp had been, there are ordeals ahead to which even Mrs. Moore may be insufficient. . . .

Late in the novel, long after her death, the wasp returns, or rather it is now the idea of the wasp. The Brahman Godbole, at the climactic moment in the book, is attempting union with the divine. He does so in a ceremony that could satisfy no Western person. . . . Having impelled Mrs. Moore triumphantly to her place, he tried again. "His senses grew thinner, he remembered a wasp seen he forgot where, perhaps on a stone. He loved the wasp equally, he impelled it likewise, he was imitating God."

Just what is achieved by the recurrence of the wasp? To have shown Godbole triumphantly impelling Mrs. Moore would have established the effect that is most obviously needed: that of an affinity between Godbole and the old Englishwoman who has not come so far as he along the mystical path. . . .

The recurrence of the wasp points to an identity in the objects to which the analogous characters were drawn. That each should have been powerfully attracted to something so apparently trivial as a wasp suggests that they were not only alike but mysteriously alike. . . . It can be said of the wasp as E. M. Forster said of Vinteuil's music that it has a life of its own, that it is almost an actor in the novel but not quite.[131]

One feature, the tank at Mau, has received a number of most interesting interpretations. Because it presents a universal symbol—water—in the traditional manner—as life enhancing—little controversy has surrounded the meaning of the tank. Instead, critics have been free to build up a body of useful readings. Because sacred images are committed to the waters, the tank has an almost

131. Brown, "Rhythm in the Novel," pp. 93–96.

"religious sanctity," according to V. A. Shahane.[132] Pedersen also emphasizes the sacred quality of the tank. Tracing the beneficent symbolism of water, he concludes that the capsizing of the boats into the tide produces "a great baptism into rebirth."[133] Elsie Leach agrees: "The scene realizes, on the Anglo-Indian level, the rebirth by water which is the concern of the Temple section. The outsiders are overturned because Stella draws back in confusion from the servitor-borne sacred tray, whose disappearance in the waters signals the closing of the gates of salvation. But not before the outsiders too are purified. The letters of Ronny and Adela, falling from Aziz's pocket in the crush, float off like the other scape-goats tossed in the tank, and can no longer keep Aziz and Fielding apart." The outsiders, she continues, return to the watery element and participate in the ceremony itself. Thus the principals are brought together within the framework of the larger meeting of nature and spirit.[134] Miss Leach's likening of the incident to one of God's practical jokes on man recalls Forster's remarks on the Hindu ritual at Mau: "By sacrificing good taste, this worship achieved what Christianity has shirked: the inclusion of merriment."[135]

Since the majority of scholars writing about *A Passage to India* agree that the novel offers both realistic social criticism, largely by satiric means, and symbolic representations of metaphysical theses, the questions arise: How well do these two planes operate together to indicate a

132. Shahane, "Symbolism in E. M. Forster's *A Passage to India:* 'Temple,'" p. 429.

133. Pedersen, "Forster's Symbolic Form," p. 244.

134. Elsie Leach, "Forster's *A Passage to India*," *Explicator* XIII (October 1954), 13.

135. E. M. Forster, *A Passage to India* (New York: Harcourt, Brace & Co., 1924), p. 289.

whole world and how successful is Forster in the dual roles of satirist and symbolist?

Brown was one of the first critics to raise the problem of the development of realistic character in a novel of ideas such as *A Passage to India*.[136] But as early as 1927, even before his article, the issue of the two levels had been discussed publicly in an essay by Virginia Woolf. Mrs. Woolf criticized the book for containing "a greater accumulation of facts than the imagination is able to deal with," and she is probably thinking of Forster's imagination as well as the reader's.[137] Other critics with a less subtle habit of mind have accused Forster outright of a failure of skill. Cecil charges that "he does not, for all his art, always succeed in harmonizing realism and symbolism."[138] A number of critics who have expressed great admiration for the novel see this split as a problem. Thus, White writes of the "crack between the comic manner and the cosmic meaning,"[139] and Hardy faults Forster for subordinating "plausible action and psychology to an idealogical pattern."[140] Crews finds this same shortcoming; Forster's characters have the air of being created to animate a preconceived plan: "That Forster's novels are thematically coherent is admirable, of course, but we would prefer that the themes appear to grow out of the characters rather than the reverse."[141]

But Forster has supporters as well who believe that he

136. E. K. Brown, "The Revival of E. M. Forster," pp. 668–81.

137. Woolf, "The Novels of E. M. Forster," p. 648. Had she offered a solution according to her own novelistic practice, Mrs. Woolf might have suggested removing all the material that could not be transformed into symbols through the novelist's vision. But Forster, in all likelihood deliberately, leaves some of his facts to act as persuaders that simulated Chandrapore is a surrogate of the real world.

138. Cecil, "E. M. Forster," p. 63.

139. White, "*A Passage to India*: Analysis and Revaluation," p. 655.

140. Hardy, *The Appropriate Form: An Essay on the Novel*, p. 75.

141. Crews, *The Perils of Humanism*, p. 174.

has managed to weave the two strands of the novel into one pattern. Dickinson wrote to him: "Whereas in your other books your kind of double vision squints—this world and a world or worlds behind—here it all comes together."[142] And Hardy makes an exception of Mrs. Moore, at least, in her charge that Forster's ideology cramps his people's psychological development. She writes that Mrs. Moore's "virtues are properly enacted, so that we respond not to an idea but to an individual portrait. She is shown in action and change."[143] Some critics find that the characters are large enough for the plot but cannot support the burden of the metaphysical theme: Trilling wants "a larger Englishman than Fielding, a weightier Indian than Aziz."[144] For White the people are either too small, like Aziz, or never really satisfactory as human beings like Godbole and Mrs. Moore.[145] But Enright suggests that the characters are deliberately small in scale to allow India itself to assume the largest possible symbolic role: "I wonder whether larger Englishmen and weightier Indians would have helped towards a more sensitive and cogent exploration of the Indian situation. . . . Perhaps it would be nearer to the point to say that the author's powers of characterization are at work elsewhere, that the great character in the book is India herself (who, as Forster stresses, is too big, too elusive, to possess what

142. Forster, *Goldsworthy Lowes Dickinson*, p. 216. See also Harry T. Moore, *E. M. Forster* in which he praises *A Passage to India* because the people fuse with the theme and plot (p. 37).

143. Hardy, *The Appropriate Form: An Essay on the Novel*, p. 76. In defense of this judgment, Miss Hardy elucidates the character of Mrs. Moore: "[She] is convincingly detached and irritable in her relations with her son Ronny and Adela even before she goes into the Marabar cave for her experience of vastation" (p. 76). Miss Hardy does not subscribe to the theory of Mrs. Moore's supernal knowledge: "Her wisdom is unmysterious good plain common sense [and] consistent respect for all creatures" (p. 77).

144. Trilling, *E. M. Forster*, p. 147.

145. White, *"A Passage to India:* Analysis and Revaluation," p. 654.

we call 'character'), and that the human characters cannot but dwindle against this vast amorphous Anti-character—and dwindle in the direction of types or even caricatures."[146] Tallying the answers to the question of whether the realistic and symbolic elements cohere in the novel reveals an almost even split, with Forster's defenders slightly more numerous and far more ardent.

How, then, has Forster fared at the hands of the critics? They have treated him well. His stock has always been high with scholars and they have considered his book conscientiously, at worst; sensitively, at best. All of the major issues that the novel raises have found at least a few interpreters. If it continues to soar beyond the reach of its most spirited analysts, that is because art always transcends criticism.

146. Enright, *The Apothecary's Shop*, pp. 183, 184.

5. *A Passage to India:*
An Interpretation

Nor mouth had, no nor mind, expressed
What heart heard of, ghost guessed
                    Gerard Manley Hopkins

IN "The Raison d'Etre of Criticism in the Arts," Forster
writes, "I would like to discover some spiritual parity
between [criticism] and the object it criticises."[1] With the
exception of those writers sympathetic toward and
knowledgeable about Hinduism, Forster's critics have
been, for the most part, too logical, too conventional, too
burdened with a different set of assumptions to have their
interpretations achieve a close rapport with the work they
were examining. Even when reading *A Passage to India*
closely, they have expected a tidy and consistent schematization and an endorsement of the philosophic views
held by one of the major characters. But Forster's

---

1. Forster, "The Raison d'Etre of Criticism in the Arts," in *Two Cheers
for Democracy*, p. 113. This essay appeared for the first time in 1947 under a
different title.

intention is different: "I tried to indicate the human predicament in a universe which is not, so far, comprehensible to our minds."[2] The predicament facing the characters in the novel can be summed up as their desire for connection, for union in a world where separation and dissolution are ever present and rarely understood.

The desire for union manifests itself differently in the various characters: when she lands in India, Mrs. Moore aspires "to be one with the universe" (p. 208). "The song of the future must transcend creed," Aziz decides in a moment of vision (p. 268). Godbole, who himself desires union with Brahman, says about another of Aziz's poems, one on the brotherhood of nations, "Ah, that is bhakti" (p. 293).[3] Fielding and Adela do not seek "an infinite goal behind the stars" (p. 264), but they desire connection with their fellow men. Throughout the book, the characters call to the Moslem Friend, the Hindu Krishna, nature, mankind, the universe, but no response seems forthcoming. Caste, religion, nationality, race, and individual perversity join a silent universe in keeping men alone and unsatisfied. Yet they continue to seek and, amazingly, some limited connection is made. *A Passage to India* poses the question: Is a fulfilling union with Godhead or mankind possible? The answer is part of the author's conception of reality and he chose to use India not only as the novel's setting, but as a testing ground for that reality.

India appealed powerfully to Forster. He disliked the changes that industrialism was making in England, although he saw them as inevitable; and he was unimpressed with the claims of science or politics as

2. From a program note for the dramatization of *A Passage to India*, quoted by Santha Rama Rau, the playwright, in Natwar Singh, *E. M. Forster*, p. 50.

3. *Bhakti* means "devotion," "self-surrender." Godbole considers Aziz's poem to have been written in such a spirit and to be capable of inspiring it in other readers.

warranting a civilized man's prime attention.[4] India offered land—vast and extraordinary. Forster always had an amateur's interest in geology, as is evidenced by the introductory chapter of "Caves": occasionally he speculated about a particular physical environment's determination of the character of its people.[5] Unmechanized India offered him its awesome longevity, the ancient traditions of its religion and art, and an unswerving insistence on the elemental forms of existence—both human and nonhuman. In India, basic matters could be understood better, especially that the certainties of Forster's Western heritage were empty: "All the small change of the north rang false," he says, "and nothing remained certain but the dome of the sky and the disc of the sun."[6] And Forster writes in the manuscript of the novel: "India offers us nothing when we question her, not even the certainty of Hell."[7]

The physical elements of the Indian nonhuman world play a dominant role in the novel's representation of the conflict between union and separation. Although the trees are stronger "than man or his works," it is the vast sky that "settles everything. . . . When the sky chooses, glory can rain into the Chandrapore bazaars or a benediction pass from horizon to horizon. The sky can do this because it is so strong and enormous." This strength "comes from the sun, infused in it daily; size from the prostrate earth," but the sky connects everything.[8] In the Marabar Hills, "it dominated as usual" (p. 141). The

4. See, for instance, E. M. Forster, "The Ivory Tower," *Atlantic Monthly* CLXIII (January 1939), 51.

5. The introduction to *Pharos and Pharillon*, for example, reveals Forster's geological concerns.

6. Forster, "Adrift in India," in *Abinger Harvest*, p. 288. This essay appeared for the first time in 1914.

7. Harrison, "The Manuscript," p. 267.

8. These quotations are from the novel's first chapter, in which the mythic qualities of sky, sun, and earth are immediately established.

earth, prostrate beneath the sky, seems hostile toward man: it "tries to keep men in compartments;" it was as if "irritation exuded from the very soil." Venice can claim a "harmony between the works of man and the earth that upholds them," but in India, "there is something hostile in [the] soil."[9] The sun, too, appears "treacherous"; the agent of "disillusionment," "he was not the unattainable friend,[10] either of men or birds or other suns, he was not the eternal promise, the never-withdrawn suggestion that haunts our consciousness; he was merely a creature like the rest, and so debarred from glory" (pp. 211, 115).

The significance of the Indian elements can be considered either in the light of the malevolent power they exert over man which leads to difficulties and separation,[11] or that of their being "creatures," like man, in Forster's cosmogony. A person taking the latter view might attempt a harmonious, if submissive, relation with the nonhuman components of the universe since all "creatures" comprise creation and may equally be the stuff of creation. This idea, which accords with Hinduism, can also be put into a secular context: Forster believes that man should attempt to dominate man-made machines but should try to adapt himself to natural phenomena.[12] Consider the stones of India. Mr. Sorley, the missionary who grows uneasy at the thought of admitting wasps into heaven, surely rejects stones. Godbole, during his religious

9. Forster, *A Passage to India*, pp. 127, 78, 282, 18.

10. See my discussion of the Friend in Chapter 2, pp. 53–56.

11. In the novel's final paragraph, neither earth nor sky wants Fielding and Aziz to be friends.

12. Forster, who rarely concerns himself with "should," has written that the natives of Devi "were civilised, they were in accord with their surroundings, they were not struggling to adjust themselves against time, like the doomed westerner" ("Woodlanders on Devi," *New Statesman and Nation*, n.s. XVII [May 6, 1939], 679).

ecstasy at Mau, tries to encompass the stone but fails. Forster's authorial voice records at the Marabar: "The boulders said, 'I am alive,' the small stones answered, 'I am almost alive'" (p. 151). And later: "How indeed is it possible for one human being to be sorry for all the sadness that meets him on the face of the earth, for the pain that is endured not only by men, but by animals and plants, and perhaps by the stones?" (p. 247). Forster is not being whimsical here.[13] He is considering in the limits of human awareness a limitation which may prevent man from comprehending the nature of reality.

If, however, the critic should pattern a neat, moral scheme for the sun, sky, earth, stars, and stones, Forster will bring him up short; one reads in "Temple," for example, that "the friendly sun of the monsoons shone forth and flooded the world with colour" (p. 305). The sun is not really hostile, the caves turn out not to be really final, the darkness is never really absolute. Forster goes beyond an advocacy of relativism. Interwoven with the initial duality of separation and union is a second duality: the manifestation of all things, under the veil of illusion (the Hindu maya)[14] seemingly permanent, is actually transient, while, beneath the surface, man can catch a glimmer of an unattainable absolute which is posited as Truth. This doctrine also sounds much like orthodox Hinduism. Howsoever that may be, it informs the novel

13. F. R. Leavis thinks he is. Leavis complains that "so fine a writer should be able, in such a place, to be so little certain just how serious he is" (*The Common Pursuit* [London: Chatto & Windus, 1952], p. 274).

14. "*Māyā*, from the root *mā*, 'to measure, to form, to build,' denotes, in the first place, the power of a god or demon to produce illusory effects, to change form, and to appear under deceiving masks. Derived from this is the meaning, 'magic,' the production of an illusion by supernatural means; and then, simply, 'the production of an illusion'. . . . Sankara describes the entire visible cosmos as *māyā*, an illusion superimposed upon true being by man's deceitful senses and unilluminated mind" (Zimmer, *Philosophies of India*, p. 19n).

and completes, with Forsterian tentativeness, the picture of man's predicament: separation may be caused by mistaking illusion for reality; union might come were man able to recognize the single, stable power in all things.

Forster created two particularly vivid examples of illusion for *A Passage to India:* one—the snake-stump—he retained in the novel; the other—the raging green tree of the Marabar Hills—he developed only in a rough draft. The piece of rope lying in the road which is perceived as a snake is one of the classic Vedantic examples of maya. But Forster actually had, at Devi, the experience of seeing a snake that turned out upon closer examination to be a tree stump. Of this incident, he wrote, "Everything that happens is said to be one thing and proves to be another, and as it is further said in an unknown tongue I live in a haze."[15] In the novel, shortly before a trick of perception replaces the withered palm stump with a snake, Forster has written of the landscape: "Everything seemed cut off at its root, and therefore infected with illusion" (p. 140). The case of the green tree in the MS is even more explicit. Fielding goes off to see a cave and, in the glare of the sun on the granite, he spies a raging green tree:

> But it brought no solace, it was too isolated and odd. What was a tree doing in that brazier? What compact had it made, and with whom? Fielding . . . avoided this brilliantly lighted vegetable, whose roots appeared to sink straight into the granite. It seemed to him that it was up to no good. Just as he had accepted his surroundings and thought "Very well: let everything be rock," it cried "No: the matter is not nearly so simple" and removed a support from his mind. "You want a mystery," it waved: "human beings do, but I announce

15. *The Hill of Devi*, p. 93. A similar instance of mutability and transience is recorded in the novel in connection with the little green bird that Ronny and Adela fail to label: "But nothing in India is identifiable, the mere asking of a question causes it to disappear or to merge in something else" (p. 86).

no mystery, only a muddle; the universe, incompre-
hensible to your reason, shall yet offer no repose
to your soul." And when he climbed above it and
looked back, it resembled neither a tree nor a rock, but
ordure.[16]

Just when Fielding has formed the idea of a harsh, sterile
landscape, the pattern is broken by the verdant tree. But
as soon as his mind has accommodated this new fact, he
discovers that, from another vantage point, the tree has
assumed a totally different aspect. Forster did not use this
passage in his final draft—probably because the treatment
is a bit heavy-handed and only repeats what the snake-
stump incident has established—but this excerpt and the
one he did retain reveal that he judged illusion to be an
essential part of the world his novel was projecting.

The rough drafts of the novel are also helpful in furthering an understanding of that single, unrealizable, ultimate
power which Forster thinks may lie beyond the transient
movement of the world. A comparison of a key passage in
the novel—the casting of the tray bearing the figures of the
Krishna birth story onto the waters of the tank at Mau
during the Gokul Ashtami festival—with an earlier
version Forster created but then edited will show the draft
explicating the published passage and both excerpts
illuminating the core of *A Passage to India*.

[The novel:] Thus was He thrown year after year, and
were others thrown—little images of Ganpati, baskets of
ten-day corn, tiny tazias after Mohurram—scapegoats,
husks, emblems of passage, a passage not easy, not now,
not here, not to be apprehended except when it is
unattainable: the God to be thrown was an emblem of
that. [pp. 314–15]

[MS. A:] Thus was He thrown year after year, and

16. Harrison, "The Manuscript," p. 336. The duality of muddle and
mystery raised in this passage will soon be considered.

were others thrown—little images of Ganpati, baskets of ten-day corn, tiny tazias after Mohurram—scapegoats, husks, emblems of salvation, a salvation not easy, not now, not here where the earth says "be different" from the start of time, not to be apprehended except when it is unattainable: the God to be thrown was an emblem of that. Why this sacrifice [Forster also thought of using "rapid destruction" instead of "sacrifice"] at the heart of creation? To ask this question is to be sensible, but none who asks it will make passage to India. [p. 699]

The unpublished version reinforces the impression one receives from the novel: the emblems of passage are man's surrogates in an ardently desired union. Under the torrent of rain, awash on the waters of the tank, the various dolls float into one another—evil "King Kansa was confounded with the father and mother of the Lord" (p. 315). When, at the end of a far longer journey, his clay melts into the divine spirit, man shall be saved. India is the ground of passage because here no distraction hinders the required concentration. Professor Godbole "picked up a fragment of the mud adhering [to the returned tray] and smeared it on his forehead without much ceremony" (p. 316). But individualism, the satisfying sense of owning a unique personality, still impedes the flow. And still the vision is animated by longing. Should passage be attained, man's apprehension of it would be transformed into another mode; man's present conception is formed by deprivation. Not to see the connection between the journey, even though it destroy the husk, and the hope such a journey creates is to miss the force not only of the metaphor but of the possibility of a power that makes union attainable.[17]

Forster, who enjoys the graphic representation of an

17. The Trimurti, the Hindu trinity—Brahma, the Creator; Vishnu, the Preserver; Siva, the Destroyer (or Dissolver)—are but three aspects of Brahman, the holy power.

ontological dilemma,[18] has created in *A Passage to India* an emblem for the endless circles of apparent reality and the barely glimpsed absolute that may lie beyond. The duality is conceived as a series of arches with the possibility of an ultimate sky overarching all. Analogous to this visual symbolization is the aural image of an endlessly coiling echo with, perhaps, an ultimate silence beyond. The concept is also given other shapes in the novel, but the principle remains constant: seeming absolutes turn out to be temporary, replaced by others, but the sought after ultimate may yet be there. The fullest expression of this idea occurs at the Bridge Party that Collector Turton gives—but not in good faith—to "bridge" the chasm between East and West: "Some kites hovered overhead, impartial, over the kites passed the mass of a vulture, and with an impartiality exceeding all, the sky, not deeply coloured but translucent, poured light from its whole circumference. It seemed unlikely that the series stopped here. Beyond the sky must not there be something that overarches all the skies, more impartial even than they? Beyond which again . . ." (pp. 39–40. The ellipsis is Forster's).[19] Here the implication is that all is in flux, that nothing will finally connect or resolve the circles. But a little later Forster writes: "Outside the arch there seemed always an arch, beyond the remotest echo a silence" (p.

18. See, for example, George Emerson's "sheet of paper on which was scrawled an enormous note of interrogation. Nothing more." When Lucy Honeychurch finds this question mark pinned over the washstand, she responds to George's questioning of the entire universe much as Mrs. Moore reacts to the echo in the Marabar: "Meaningless at first, it gradually became menacing, obnoxious, portentous with evil" (*A Room with a View*, p. 16).

19. Again, the rough drafts of the novel throw some interesting light on the published work. In one version, instead of the sky's being described as "impartial," Forster calls it "passionless," and instead of "something that overarches all the skies," he has written, "something invisible, nameless, overarching"—emphasizing the idea of some cosmic power beyond the heavens (Harrison, "The Manuscript," p. 64).

52). The first part of this sentence repeats the image of the endless arch which Forster obviously wants to stress; the second part, however, offers the view that beyond the cycles of form and movement, action and consequence, lies something totally other. Perhaps this silence is the "spiritual silence" that the visitors discover when they enter the Marabar Hills (p. 140); perhaps it is also the "absolute silence" which falls when Professor Godbole finishes his song asking Krishna to come (p. 80). Whether the final silence, the ultimate sky, promises indifference—as the Marabar Caves suggest—or peace—as the festival at Mau implies—will be considered shortly. For the present, a closer examination of the imagery of the circles which describe false absolutes.

When Ronny and Adela accept a ride in the Nawab Bahadur's new automobile, they have become estranged as a result of their different attitudes about India and Indians. Yet, in the car, their hands touch by accident, the physical contact stirs them, and their differences are reconciled. Forster writes of this touch of hands: "Each was too proud to increase the pressure, but neither withdrew it, and a spurious unity descended on them, as local and temporary as the gleam that inhabits a firefly. It would vanish in a moment, perhaps to reappear, but the darkness is alone durable. And the night that encircled them, absolute as it seemed, was itself only a spurious unity, being modified by the gleams of day that leaked up around the edges of the earth, and by the stars" (p. 88). The reader's position is similar to Fielding's at the advent of the raging green tree. Just when he has accepted the view that the connection between Ronny and Adela is temporary and that only the darkness itself is permanent, Forster announces that the night itself is a false absolute, dependent upon the sun's light which encircles it. But perhaps beyond the sun is an engulfing darkness.

The nihilism which Mrs. Moore discovers in the Marabar Caves and which she understands as the ultimate message of India also turns out to be just one of the arches through which experience passes. As her boat sails out of the Bombay Harbor, the cocoanut palms "wave her farewell. 'So you thought an echo was India; you took the Marabar caves as final?' they laughed. 'What have we in common with them, or they with Asirgarh? Goodbye!'" (p. 210). Mrs. Moore knows her visit has been inconclusive; she has "not seen the right places" (p. 209). But neither Bombay nor Asirgarh would be final either. Aziz has a similar insight when he meets Mrs. Moore's son Ralph and finds that the lesson of separation which the caves had taught him was final is dissolving into a desire for friendship like that he felt when he first met Mrs. Moore in the mosque: "Never be friends with English! Mosque, caves, mosque, caves. And here he was starting again" (p. 311).

All of India is seen as radiating in wider and wider circles, no one more real than the others. One circle is comprised of the Indian pleaders, who press their clients' cases. The clients themselves comprise another circle: "And there were circles even beyond these—people who wore nothing but a loincloth, people who wore not even that, and spent their lives in knocking two sticks together before a scarlet doll—humanity grading and drifting beyond the educated vision, until no earthly invitation can embrace it" (p. 37). The same idea recurs on the train ride to the Marabar Hills: "The branch line stops, the road is only practicable for cars to a point, the bullock-carts lumber down the side tracks, paths fray out into the cultivation, and disappear near a splash of red paint. How can the mind take hold of such a country?" (p. 136).

Where, then, can the "real" India that Adela Quested

is seeking be found among the arches and echoes? Forster has written: "I don't myself like the phrase 'the real India.' I suspect it. It always makes me prick up my ears."[20] In the novel, Aziz tells Adela, "Nothing embraces the whole of India, nothing, nothing" (p. 145).[21] Sometimes Aziz feels he owns "the land as much as anyone owned it" (p. 23), but Fielding knows that "it's nobody's India" (p. 277). Elsewhere, Forster has noted, "there are so many [Indias]; and each pilgrim finds the shrine he seeks."[22] Indeed, there are "a hundred Indias" (p. 15).[23] Yet when the point has been established beyond doubt, Forster suggests, during a conversation between Adela and Fielding, "Perhaps the hundred Indias which fuss and squabble so tiresomely are one, and the universe they mirror is one" (p. 263). Perhaps, in short, despite the apparent differences, there is unity; perhaps, beyond the arches, there is a final, overarching sky.

20. Forster, "India Again," in *Two Cheers for Democracy*, p. 321. Under a different title, this essay first appeared in 1946. Cf. Harrison, "The Manuscript": "Words like 'real'. . . . carried no weight with Mrs. Moore: she was too old" (p. 189).

21. "In her ignorance [Adela] regarded [Aziz] as 'India,' and never surmised that his outlook was limited and his method inaccurate, and that no one is India" (p. 72).

22. E. M. F[orster], "Indian Caves," review of *My Pilgrimages to Ajanta and Bagh* by S. M. C. Dey, *Nation and Athenaeum*, July 11, 1925, p. 462.

23. This idea is not an unusual one; only Forster's use of it in the larger metaphysical scheme is original. Sir Valentine Chirol has written: "We have got too much into the habit of talking about India and the Indians as if they were one country and one people, and we too often forget that there are far more absolutely distinct languages spoken in India than in Europe; between the Mahratta and the Bengalee than between the German and the Portuguese, between the Punjabee and the Tamil than between the Russian and the Italian; that, not to speak of other creeds, the religious antagonism between Hindu and Mohomedan is often more active than any that exists to-day between Protestants and Roman Catholics, even, let us say, in Ulster; and that caste has driven into Indian society lines of far deeper cleavage than any class distinctions that have survived in Europe" (*Indian Unrest*, p. 323).

And what is the nature of this absolute? In *The Longest Journey*, his second novel, Forster considers the same problem, creates a graphic image to express it, and finds no complete answer. Rickie Elliot's friend Ansell is given to drawing a certain figure: "Ansell was sitting alone with a piece of paper in front of him. On it was a diagram—a circle inside a square, inside which was again a square" (p. 17). Here is the same concept as the never ending arch, the ever sounding echo, except that, instead of radiating outward, Ansell's diagram moves toward the center. As he continues to draw circles inside squares inside circles, Rickie asks:

> "Why will you do that?"
> No answer.
> "Are they real?"
> "The inside one is—the one in the middle of everything, that there's never room enough to draw." [p. 19]

The universe is, indeed, "not, so far, comprehensible to our minds."

Yet Forster does attempt in *A Passage to India* to envision the reality there is never room enough to draw. He offers two versions: the Marabar Hills and the religious celebration at Mau.

The salient feature of the Marabar Hills is that they offer another Forsterian duality: the caves and the echo. For although critics often use "Caves" generically to include both phenomena, Forster treats these two features of the hills very differently. The caves are neutral; the echo is evil. The long introduction to the caves emphasizes that they are utterly without moral attributes. Writing of the as yet unopened caves, Forster says: "Nothing is inside them, they were sealed up before the creation of pestilence or treasure; if mankind grew curious and excavated, nothing, nothing would be added to the sum of good or evil" (p. 125). And of all the caves, he insists: "Nothing, nothing attaches to them, and their reputation—for they have one—does not depend upon human speech. It is as if the surrounding plain or the passing birds have taken upon themselves to exclaim 'extraordinary,' and the word has taken root in the air, and been inhaled by mankind" (p. 124). The caves predate the logical and ethical distinctions human speech has made possible; they have witnessed the creation of the world. The echo, however, is associated with people and is called evil: it is the effect of the caves' indifference on human beings. Thus Adela, the echo continuing to buzz in her ears after her nightmare in the Marabar, believes it to be somehow pernicious: "The sound had spouted after her when she escaped, and was going on still like a river that gradually floods the plain. Only Mrs. Moore could drive it back to its source and seal the broken reservoir. Evil was loose . . . she could even hear it entering the lives of others" (p. 194. The ellipsis is Forster's). In one rough draft of the novel, Forster specifically mentions that the unopened, unentered caves have no echo.[24] The caves existed before mankind, but the echo is man-made. Forster does not suggest that mankind—or even some men—are inherently evil. The sounds people make in the caves may be completely innocuous; it is the words bouncing off the granite walls that produce the disturbing echo: "Everything echoes now; there's no stopping the echo. The original sound may be harmless, but the echo is always evil" (p. 276). These are Fielding's thoughts and they are valid because the original sound of Adela's fingernail scratching on the granite is totally harmless, but the echo it generates ultimately causes the incarceration of Aziz and leads to the estrangement between Aziz and Fielding. Although the evil does not stop even there, it must not be

24. Harrison, "The Manuscript," p. 241.

viewed as inherent in the nature of the caves. In the last chapter of the book, it is suggested that the evil of the Marabar is wiped out: the echo was a bitter illusion. The reality of the caves, however, remains: the principle of the universe is not individuation but the single spirit common to all things.

For Mrs. Moore and Adela, the idea that there are no distinct categories is an evil one and their response is a kind of resistance. Mrs. Moore's subsequent withdrawal is a way of asserting the self; Adela's hallucination that she has been attacked, already considered in Chapter 3, is a parody of the concept of nondifferentiation. The imagery of the Marabar which encompasses the two women is mostly negative—colored by bleakness, dissatisfaction, and separation.[25] The reader learns that what has spoken to Mrs. Moore in the cave is "something very old and very small. Before time, it was before space also. Something snub-nosed, incapable of generosity—the undying worm itself" (p. 208). For Mrs. Moore the idea that everything is one reduces itself to the formula that it's all nothing.[26] In one early draft, Forster had used, instead of the phrase, "the undying worm itself," the term, "the spectre of pettiness."[27] Mrs. Moore, who has "desired to be one with the universe," decides in the Marabar that a universe not ruled by a just and merciful God is small and horrible—

25. One such image is the match which is struck near the polished wall of a cave: "Immediately another flame rises in the depths of the rock and moves towards the surface like an imprisoned spirit. . . . The two flames approach and strive to unite, but cannot, because one of them breathes air, the other stone. . . . The radiance increases, the flames touch one another, kiss, expire" (p. 125). Abortive versions in the MS read: "touch one another," "desire to kiss," "die of a kiss," or "die with kissing" (p. 738). Like the appeal to the Friend, like the call to Krishna, the flames seek the union beyond illusion, but only the ensuing darkness joins them.

26. "We must exclude someone from our gathering, or we shall be left with nothing," Mr. Sorley thinks, in denying the lower orders entrance to heaven (p. 38).

27. Harrison, "The Manuscript," p. 456.

petty, in fact, and her behavior after this discovery becomes itself petty, as if she had met in the cave the principle of self in its narrowest form.[28] India has intensified her predicament: separated from her Christian God, she cannot love anyone.

Mrs. Moore is suffering from "spiritual muddledom" (p. 208)—the self-delusion that results in loss of connection.[29] But the problem of muddle is not only Mrs. Moore's: it concerns the other characters and India itself. Fielding tells the old lady that India is really a muddle, not a "mystery" as she had hoped; in fact, Fielding holds that a "mystery is only a high-sounding term for a muddle" (p. 69). When he thus labels India, Fielding means that, unlike the Mediterranean civilization which "has escaped muddle" (p. 282), India does not satisfy his need for form, pattern—a connection between things. And nowhere is muddle greater than in the Marabar Hills. But that is their truth: while form creates and clarifies distinctions—distinctions which are relative, temporary, misleading—muddle erases barriers and shows the interrelatedness of creation. Despite the misconceptions about their meaning which separate creatures, the Marabar Caves, with their spiritual silence beyond the sounds and echoes of men, like the white radiance behind the colors of the world, prefigure the ultimate reality.

"Temple" offers a related conception of the spirit that lies beyond the final arch. Like the Marabar, the festival at Mau is a "muddle (as we call it), a frustration of reason and form" (p. 285). But Forster's aside makes it clear that only the uninitiated characterize the mystery as muddle. "God is Love" will do as well as any version since

28. Mrs. Moore has not encountered the Hindu Atman, the holy power in the aspect of its personal indwelling, but rather the individual will, which isolates as it asserts itself.

29. Cf. Forster, *A Room with a View*, p. 236 and *Howards End*, p. 308.

"whatever can be stated must be temporary."[30] Nevertheless, "Temple" is a statement of unity, a unity which it can be hoped mirrors the absolute.

Most critics of *A Passage to India* have noticed the joyousness of the novel's final section, but many have underestimated its pervasiveness because it does not affect the outcome of the plot very greatly. For Forster, however, human beings are only one of a host of elements in the cosmos. Much of the unity expressed in "Temple" has nothing to do with the characters. Consider the three aspects of God in the first paragraph: he is about to be born in the Gokul Ashtami ritual; he was born centuries ago—as the Krishna whose birth has been recorded in the Puranas; he can never be born because, as an incarnation of Vishnu who is himself an aspect of Brahman, he is eternal. Yet the God is one.

And Godbole who participates in the ceremony is himself both God and supplicant: "It was his duty, as it was his desire, to place himself in the position of the God and to love [Mrs. Moore], and to place himself in her position and to say to the God, 'Come, come, come, come'" (pp. 290–91). His soul, impelling hers, is just one "tiny reverberation" (p. 286) of the whole. As Hindu scripture has it, mankind is one of the gestures in the divine power's cosmic dance.

All the elements fuse at Mau, even the sounds of man and nature: "Music there was, but from so many sources that the sum-total was untrammelled. The braying banging crooning melted into a single mass which trailed round the palace before joining the thunder" (p. 284). When Aziz rides over to visit the guest house the next evening, he examines the great tank: "Reflecting the evening clouds, it filled the nether-world with an equal splendour, so that earth and sky leant toward one another,

30. Forster notes this Hindu idea in "The Gods of India," p. 338.

about to clash in ecstasy" (p. 306). As with the match
and its reflection, this union cannot actually take place,
but the desire is seen as beautiful in itself. During the
festival, "All sorrow was annihilated," for the human and
nonhuman as well (p. 287). When a prisoner is released
from the local jail, a rocket is sounded, and it is as if this
release symbolizes mankind's hopes to be saved. So
profound is the spirit of communion at Mau that the
villagers temporarily lose their individuality and come to
resemble one another: "When the villagers broke cordon
for a glimpse of the silver image, a most beautiful and
radiant expression came into their faces, a beauty in
which there was nothing personal, for it caused them all to
resemble one another during the moment of its indwelling, and only when it was withdrawn did they
revert to individual clods" (p. 284).

   At the climax, Aziz and Ralph, Fielding and Stella,
boating on the tank to witness the casting of the replica
of the village of Gokul onto the waters, become partici-
pants, of a sort, in the ceremony. The boats collide: "The
four outsiders flung out their arms and grappled, and,
with oars and poles sticking out, revolved like a mythical
monster in the whirlwind. The worshippers howled with
wrath or joy, as they drifted forward helplessly against the
servitor" (p. 315). In a moment the boats capsize and
everything floats out onto the water, including the letters
from Ronny and Adela to the Fieldings which Aziz has
filched during his trip to the guest house: "The oars, the
sacred tray, the letters of Ronny and Adela, broke loose
and floated confusedly" (p. 315). These letters are more
important than has usually been realized; they reveal to
Aziz that the English are making up their differences with
one another. Adela's letter, especially, is full of a warm
and friendly spirit. In the last chapter, Aziz shows Fielding
a letter *he* has written to Adela—a letter of forgiveness and

even praise: "As I fell into our largest Mau tank ... I thought how brave Miss Quested was and decided to tell her so" (p. 317). Perhaps Adela's friendly letter, floating among the other emblems of passage, rekindles the desire for union with his fellow men which Aziz's meeting with Ralph Moore has already stirred. In his letter, Aziz tells Adela: "For my own part, I shall henceforth connect you with the name that is very sacred in my mind, namely, Mrs. Moore" (p. 320). Thus, at Mau, Aziz is reunited with Adela, Fielding, and Mrs. Moore. "God is Love. Is this the first message of India?" Forster writes (p. 285).[31] He implies that it is.

Is one justified in saying, then, that the author of *A Passage to India* embraces Hindu mysticism and suggests that his readers do likewise? Both the novel itself and Forster's related writings make such a query somehow irrelevant; despite their large scope, the questions are constructed to produce answers that do not signify.

A Passage to India is largely a work of negations and silences. The ellipses leave a good deal to the discretion of the reader—which is why interpretations have been so various. The Marabar Caves are described as having nothing "attached" to them; the Hindu God is said, at the festival, to have no "attributes"; evil is understood as "God's absence"; Indian civilization is lacking in "form." The unknown is, by definition, hypothetical, and mystical states, by their very nature, do not lend themselves to verbal analyses afterwards. Despite the seeming absurdity of the quest, the chief motivation of Vedic philosophy, "from the period of even the earliest philosophic hymns ... has been, without change, the search for a basic unity

31. Cf. Forster's good friend, G. L. Dickinson, writing of *his* response to India: "is this all-comprehensive Hinduism, this universal toleration, this refusal to recognize ultimate antagonisms, this 'mush,' in a word, as my friends would dub it—is this, after all, the truest and profoundest vision?" (*Appearances*, p. 34).

underlying the manifold of the universe."[32] In India, Forster pursued the same search, but the goal is wide enough to admit of many parallel paths. "Temperamentally, I am an individualist,"[33] Forster has written, and anyone familiar with his life and work is bound to agree. He is conscious of man's instinct for both gregariousness and solitude: "We are here on earth not to save ourselves and not to save the community, but to try to save both."[34] Hinduism is concerned with neither individualism as Forster uses the word nor with saving the community.

Forster's sympathies are wide and their edges not sharply defined. He could love the Maharajah of Dewas without approving of him as a ruler and he can admire Professor Godbole without desiring to emulate him. He is more concerned with the predicaments men face than with theories concerning "should": he chides "schoolmasters and other men of good will" because "once started on the subject of Life they lose all diffidence [since] to them it is ethical. They love discussing what we ought to do instead of what we have to face."[35] In the same essay, he goes on to say that, of all games, the one most obviously resembling life is piquet:

> It is in the first place obviously and overwhelmingly unfair. Fate is dealt, despite skill in discarding, and neither in the rules of play nor in the marking is there the least attempt to redress misfortune or to give the sufferer a fresh chance. The bias is all the other way. . . . Yet this savage pastime admits the element of Free Will. It is

32. Zimmer, *Philosophies of India*, p. 338.

33. Forster, "The Challenge of our Time," p. 55.

34. Forster, "The Ivory Tower," p. 58. This is a rare instance of Forster's prescribing for the many instead of describing the code he personally follows.

35. Forster, "The Game of Life," in *Abinger Harvest*, p. 54. This essay first appeared in 1919.

possible to retard or accelerate Fate. Play, subtle and vigorous play, goes on all the time, though the player is being swept to disaster or victory by causes beyond his control, and it is in the play, rather than the result, that the real interest of the game resides.[36]

Thus, Forster is more concerned with what his characters do than with what they ought to do. He does not expect them to be larger than life any more than he expects real people to be.

Professor Godbole, like all of the characters in *A Passage to India*, partially succeeds in what he is after. He seeks union with God, not man, and his dilemma is whether Krishna will ever answer his call. In a review of W. G. Archer's *The Loves of Krishna*, Forster has written: "The infinite has enough to go round—enough and to spare."[37] But in the novel, written many years earlier, he is more pessimistic: "Trees of a poor quality bordered the road, indeed the whole scene was inferior, and suggested that the countryside was too vast to admit of excellence. In vain did each item in it call out, 'Come, come.' There was not enough god to go around" (pp. 87–88). The climax of Professor Godbole's religious devotions is reached during Gokul Ashtami. Forster describes it carefully:

Not an orgy of the body; the tradition of that shrine forbade it. But the human spirit had tried by a desperate contortion to ravish the unknown, flinging down science and history in the struggle, yes, beauty herself. Did it succeed? Books written afterwards say "Yes." But how, if there is such an event, can it be remembered afterwards? How can it be expressed in anything but itself? Not only from the unbeliever are mysteries hid, but the adept himself cannot retain them. He may think, if he chooses, that he has been with God, but as soon as he

36. Ibid., pp. 56–57.
37. Forster, "The Blue Boy," p. 444.

thinks it, it becomes history, and falls under the rules of time. [p. 288]

The famous Hindu mystic, Ramakrishna, whom Dickinson was reading during his and Forster's first trip to India,[38] has described in a parable this same difficulty of transmitting mystical experience: "In samadhi one attains the knowledge of Brahman—one realizes Brahman. In that state reasoning stops altogether and man becomes mute. He has no power to describe the nature of Brahman. Once a salt doll went to measure the depth of the ocean. It wanted to tell others how deep the water was. But this it could never do, for no sooner had it got into the water than it melted. Now who was there to speak about the depth?"[39] Limited as Godbole's vision is, he is reasonably satisfied: "'One old Englishwoman and one little, little wasp,' he thought, as he stepped out of the temple into the grey of a pouring wet morning. 'It does not seem much, still it is more than I am myself'" (p. 291).

Unlike Godbole, Mrs. Moore has sought God largely through caring about others. Thwarted by her experience in the caves, she ends her days in disillusionment. Ironically, the love she once bore Aziz and Adela retains its meaning for them, helping them after its termination, even as her influence among the Indian populace continues after her death. Of all Forster's characters the most disappointed in her goals, Mrs. Moore is yet not a failure.

Aziz seeks God—the Moslem Friend—but less intensely than Godbole desires Krishna because Aziz seeks human

38. "Seated on the tram, it was with an effort that I opened the 'Gospel' of Sri Ramakrishna. But at once my attention was arrested. This was an account by a disciple of the life and sayings of his master" (Dickinson, *Appearances*, p. 30).

39. *The Gospel of Sri Ramakrishna*, trans. Swami Nikhilananda (New York: Ramakrishna-Vivekananda Center, 1958), p. 154. This is a classical parable. There is a possibility, however, that Forster was familiar with this version.

friendship as well. Many critics have thought that the answer to the question "Is it possible to be friends with the English?" which the Moslems raise in the second chapter is unclear because of the vicissitudes of Aziz's relationship with Fielding. But the question has been resolved by another relationship—that of Aziz with Mrs. Moore. "I like Aziz, Aziz is my real friend" (p. 97), Mrs. Moore tells her son Ronny. Aziz continues to believe in her benevolence throughout, which indicates his own generosity. The doctor and Fielding are also good friends, if not by the standards that obtain in Valhalla, then at least by those that exist among men in the real world. When, from his sickbed, Aziz shows his wife's picture to Fielding, their friendship is cemented; when, during their last ride together, Fielding tells Aziz about his relationship with Stella, the cracks are mended. At the time of the trip to the caves, Aziz thinks about friendship: "It was only when Mrs. Moore or Fielding was near him that he saw further, and knew that it is more blessed to receive than to give. These two had strange and beautiful effects on him— they were his friends, his for ever, and he theirs for ever; he loved them so much that giving and receiving became one" (pp. 142–43). Because the affairs of men are always in flux, Aziz later comes to mistrust Fielding and then to reject him. But Forster believes that the spirit of love is part of the holy spirit and never dies.[40] At the end of the novel, although they must part, there is no doubt that Aziz and Fielding are friends. It is social and political conditions that prevent them from meeting again, as an original draft spells out in more detail than the novel; Fielding asks Aziz, in one version, to visit him and the doctor replies: "Perhaps some day in England, Cyril, but

40. Consider Mr. Emerson in *A Room with a View:* "It isn't possible to love and to part. You will wish that it was. You can transmute love, ignore it, muddle it, but you can never pull it out of you" (p. 237).

never in my country. We are friends again personally, but there remains my vow" (p. 708). The political argument they engage in does not alter the affection they bear each other. Fielding's remark, "Why can't we be friends now? . . . It's what I want. It's what you want" is beside the point. The whole tenor of the conversation reveals their intimacy. Even though the divisions of daily life intervene, even though the earth and sky, mirroring the disunion of hostile nations, interpose, even though Fielding and Aziz must part, the secret understanding of the heart has triumphed.

Fielding, who is an atheist, has built his life on personal relations and, although there are times throughout the book when he catches a hint of the world he has missed beyond the material world, his relationships and his life are fairly successful. Adela Quested, whose religious commitment is almost as negligible as Fielding's, has also sought a life based on connections with other human beings. But the Marabar unsettles her world and only at the end, through her letter, does the reader surmise that she has managed to build a new life in England amid her own milieu, as she has told Fielding she could. Yet Miss Quested, whose imagination is undeveloped and whose success with people is limited, is granted by Forster a strange and wonderful vision at her trial. She sees the day at the caves as she originally experienced it—just another arch, another echo—and, then, as radiated by a beauty like no other: a much finer double vision than Mrs. Moore's:

> The fatal day recurred, in every detail, but now she was of it and not of it at the same time, and this double relation gave it indescribable splendour. Why had she thought the expedition "dull"? Now the sun rose again, the elephant waited, the pale masses of the rock flowed round her and presented the first cave; she entered, and

a match was reflected in the polished walls—all beautiful and significant, though she had been blind to it at the time. . . . Her vision was of several caves. She saw herself in one, and she was also outside it, watching its entrance, for Aziz to pass in. She failed to locate him. It was the doubt that had often visited her, but solid and attractive, like the hills. [pp. 227–29]

A manuscript version adds some interesting information to this account: "She didn't recall what had happened in the ordinary sense of memory, she didn't recapture all its terrible emotions, yet she grasped it with all her being, and answered across a sort of darkness to the voice in Chandrapore. . . . She had never before except in pictures and poetry, entirely divested the world of its boredom, the veil of mediocrity, thick or thin, had blurred it" (p. 727). For a few moments, at least, life for Adela, under the light of eternity, becomes as vivid and true as art.

Little has been said so far, except by implication, about the great art of Forster's novel. The setting is vividly realized, the characters observed with much sensitivity, the story absorbing, the theme elevated—but the real genius of the work lies in the economy with which one structure serves five different aspects of the novel. The clearest example of this is the expedition to the caves and its aftermath. On the level of plot, the reader is kept in suspense about the meaning of Adela's portentous disappearance until the party returns to Chandrapore, and even then the nature of Aziz's alleged offense is only gradually revealed. Secondly, the stress on the characters' personalities which the pressure of the outing has imposed —a subject that has already been treated here and in Chapter 3—shows Forster's psychological subtlety to be impressive. The trip also affords social satire—in this case, of the Indian rather than the English community as Aziz and Mohammed Latif run their comic opera expedition.

The political aspect of the novel focuses on the racial tension which the supposed assault provokes: the ugliness of dominion is heightened by the dramatic situation. Finally, major and minor themes grow out of the action or situation at the Marabar Hills: Aziz's attempt both to revive and identify himself with Moslem tradition; Mrs. Moore's misunderstanding, through the medium of the echo, of the caves' indifference; Adela's psychic aberration resulting from the impact that the caves' suggestion of union makes on her personal problems; the symbolism of the cave itself—the silence beyond the echo. Thus Forster's novel is beautifully integrated—each aspect's development animating the others.

"I'm not sure I would be put off simply because a dilemma that I wanted to treat was insoluble, at least, I don't think I should be," Forster said in an interview in 1953.[41] He was not put off from writing *A Passage to India* because the dilemma he wanted to treat—the desire of men for union against great difficulties; the possibility that union is a metaphysical condition not to be fully comprehended by men—is not soluble. He partly circumvents the dilemma because he is concerned with "a world that asks to be noticed rather than explained."[42] Ludwig Wittgenstein, the linguistic analyst, has said of Freud's psychoanalytic theory that it is not so much an explanation as a beautiful representation. The same thing can be said of *A Passage to India*. But in certain areas a beautiful representation is the closest thing to an explanation we are likely to get.

41. Furbank and Haskell, "The Art of Fiction," p. 32.
42. Forster, "The Last of Abinger," in *Two Cheers for Democracy*, p. 362.

Bibliography of Sources Consulted

Works by E. M. Forster

The publication dates given for Forster's works refer to the editions I used. Original publication dates are mentioned in the text and notes; they can be found in all instances in B. J. Kirkpatrick's *Bibliography of E. M. Forster* (London: Rupert Hart-Davis, 1965).

Abinger Harvest. New York: Noonday Press, 1955. Meridian Books.

Alexandria: A History and a Guide. Garden City, N.Y.: Doubleday & Co., 1961. Anchor Books.

"The Art and Architecture of India." *Listener* L (September 10, 1953), 419–21.

Aspects of the Novel. New York: Harcourt, Brace & Co., 1956. Harvest Books.

"Bikaner." *Listener* XLIII (June 22, 1950), 1065.

"The Blue Boy." *Listener* LVII (March 14, 1957), 444. Book review.

"Books of the Year." *Observer*, no. 8848 (December 17, 1961), p. 22.

"The Chapel of Kings." *Listener* XLII (May 29, 1952), 885–87. Book review.

"The Churning of the Ocean." *Athenaeum*, May 21, 1920, pp. 667–68.

The Collected Tales of E. M. Forster. New York: Alfred A. Knopf, 1947.

"A Concert of Old Instruments." *Athenaeum*, July 11, 1919, p. 597.

"East and West." *Observer*, no. 8438 (February 21, 1954), p. 9. Book review.

"Entrance to an Unwritten Novel." *Listener* XL (December 23, 1948), 975–76.

"The Gods of India." *New Weekly* I (May 30, 1914), 338. Book review.

Goldsworthy Lowes Dickinson. New York: Harcourt, Brace & Co., 1934.

The Hill of Devi. New York: Harcourt, Brace & Co., 1953.

Howards End. New York: Random House, 1958. Vintage Books.

"India and the Turk." *Nation and Athenaeum* XXXI (September 30, 1922), 844–45. [Signed F.]

"Indian Caves." *Nation and Athenaeum* XXXVII (July 11, 1925), 462. [Signed EMF.] Book review.

"Indian Entries." *Encounter* XVIII (January 1962), 20–27. Also published as "Indian Entries from a Diary." Introduction by Santha Rama Rau. *Harper's* CCXXIV (February 1962), 46–52.

"The Indian Mind." *New Weekly* I (March 28, 1914), 55. Book review.

Review of *Indian Painting for the British: 1770–1880* by Mildred and W. G. Archer. *Listener* LV (January 19, 1956), 111. [Unsigned.]

"The Individual and His God." *Listener* XXIV (December 5, 1940), 801–2.

"The Ivory Tower." *Atlantic Monthly* CLXIII (January 1939), 51–58.

"Lear in India." *Listener* IL (March 26, 1953), 519. Book review.

"The Legacy of Samuel Butler." *Listener* XLVII (June 12, 1952), 955–56.

"Lelia: The Life of George Sand." *Listener* IL (June 18, 1953), 1015. Book review.

"The Long Run." *New Statesman and Nation* XVI (December 10, 1938), 971–72. Book review.

The Longest Journey. New York: Random House, 1962. Vintage Books.

"Luso-India." *Athenaeum*, August 27, 1920, p. 268. [Signed EMF.] Book review.

Marianne Thornton: A Domestic Biography. New York: Harcourt, Brace & Co., 1956.

"'The Mint' by T. E. Lawrence." *Listener* LIII (February 17, 1955), 279–80.

"Missionaries." *Athenaeum*, October 22, 1920, pp. 545–47.

Notes on Egypt. In *The Government of Egypt*. London: Labour Research Department, 1920.

Introductory and terminal notes to *Original Letters from India*, by Eliza Fay. New York: Harcourt, Brace & Co., 1925.

A Passage to India. New York: Harcourt, Brace & Co., 1924. London: J. M. Dent & Sons, Everyman's Library edition, 1942.

Pharos and Pharillon. New York: Alfred A. Knopf, 1962.

"The Poetry of Iqbal." *Athenaeum*, December 10, 1920, pp. 803–4. Book review.

"Portraits from Memory." *Listener* XLVII (July 24, 1952), 142.

"The Possessed." *Listener* XLVIII (October 9, 1952), 595–97. Book review.

"Reflections in India, 2: The Prince's Progress." *Nation and Athenaeum* XXX (January 28, 1922), 644–46. [Unsigned.]

A Room with a View. New York: Random House, 1960. Vintage Books.

"Sidling after Crabbe." *Listener* LIII (June 9, 1955), 1039–41. Book review.

"Sir Tukoji Rao Puar." *Times* (London), December 28, 1937, p. 147.

"The Temple." *Athenaeum*, September 26, 1919, p. 947. [Signed EMF.]

"Tidying India." *Listener* LI (March 11, 1954), 435–36. Book review.

"Tourism *v.* Thuggism." *Listener* LVII (January 17, 1957), 124. Book review.

"Tributes to Sir Desmond MacCarthy." *Listener* XLVII (June 26, 1952), 1031.

Two Cheers for Democracy. New York: Harcourt, Brace & World, 1951.

"A Visit to America." *Listener* LI (May 13, 1954), 831.

Where Angels Fear to Tread. New York: Random House, 1958. Vintage Books.

"Woodlanders on Devi." *New Statesmen and Nation* XVII (May 6, 1939), 679–80.

"The World Mountain." *Listener* LII (December 2, 1954), 977–78. Book review.

Secondary Sources

Ackerley, J. R. *Hindu Holiday.* rev. ed. London: Chatto & Windus, 1952.

Allen, Glen O. "Structure, Symbol, and Theme in *A Passage to India.*" *PMLA* LXX (December 1955), 934–54.

Allen, Walter. *The English Novel.* London: Phoenix House, 1954.

Anthology of Islamic Literature. Edited by James Kritzeck. New York: New American Library, 1966.

"Attempted Assassination of Viceroy." *Times* (London), December 24, 1912, pp. 4, 5, 6. Continued December 25, p. 6; December 28, p. 4; and December 29, p. 5.

Austin, Don. "The Problem of Continuity in Three Novels of E. M. Forster." *Modern Fiction Studies* VII (Autumn 1961), 217–28.

Beer, J. B. *The Achievement of E. M. Forster.* London: Chatto & Windus, 1963.

Belgion, Montgomery. "The Diabolism of Mr. E. M. Forster." *Criterion* XIV (October 1934), 54–73.

Bentley, Phyllis. "The Novels of E. M. Forster." *College English* IX (April 1948), 349–56.

Boyle, Ted E. "Adela Quested's Delusion: The Failure of Rationalism in *A Passage to India*." *College English* XXVI (March 1965), 478–80.

Bradbury, Malcolm, ed. *Forster: A Collection of Critical Essays.* Twentieth Century Views Series. Englewood Cliffs, N.J.: Prentice-Hall, 1966.

Brander, Lawrence. "E. M. Forster and India," *Review of English Literature* III (October 1962), 76–84.

Breit, Harvey. *The Writer Observed.* Cleveland: World Publishing Co., 1956.

Brower, Reuben. *The Fields of Light.* New York: Oxford University Press, 1951.

Brown, E. K. "The Revival of E. M. Forster." In *Forms of Modern Fiction*, edited by William Van O'Connor. Minneapolis: University of Minnesota Press, 1948. First published in *Yale Review* XXXII (Summer 1944), 668–81.

Brown, E. K. *Rhythm in the Novel.* Toronto: University of Toronto Press, 1950.

Burra, Peter. "The Novels of E. M. Forster." *Nineteenth Century and After* CXVI (November 1934), 581–94.

Campbell, Sandy. "Mr. Forster of King's." *Mademoiselle* LIX (June 1964), 80–81, 120–24.

Cecil, David. "E. M. Forster." *Atlantic Monthly* CLXXXIII (January 1949), 60–65.

Chaudhuri, Nirad C. "Passage to and From India." *Encounter* II (June 1954), 19–24.

Chirol, Valentine. *Indian Unrest.* London: Macmillan & Co., 1910.

Connolly, Cyril. *The Condemned Playground.* New York: Macmillan Co., 1946.

Cooperman, Stanley. "The Imperial Posture and the Shrine of Darkness: Kipling's *The Naulahka* and E. M. Forster's *A Passage to India*." *English Literature in Transition* VI (1963), 9–13.

Crews, Frederick C. *E. M. Forster: The Perils of Humanism.* Princeton, N. J.: Princeton University Press, 1962.

Daiches, David. *The Present Age in British Literature.* Bloomington: Indiana University Press, 1958.

The Dance of Shiva and Other Tales from India. Translated by Oroon Ghosh. New York: New American Library, 1965.

Dauner, Louise. "What Happened in the Cave? Reflections on *A Passage to India.*" *Modern Fiction Studies* VII (Autumn 1961), 258–70.

Davis, F. Hadland. *The Persian Mystics: Jalalu'd-Din Rumi.* London: John Murray, 1907.

Dickinson, G. Lowes. *Appearances.* Garden City, N.Y.: Doubleday, Page & Co., 1914.

Dobree, Bonamy. *The Lamp and the Lute: Studies in Six Modern Authors.* London: Clarendon Press, 1929.

Doughty, Howard N., Jr. "The Novels of E. M. Forster." *Bookman* LXXV (October 1932), 542–49.

Drew, Elizabeth. *The Modern Novel.* New York: Harcourt, Brace & Co., 1926.

Eapen, Karippacheril Chakko. "E. M. Forster and India." Ph.D. dissertation, University of Colorado, 1962.

Enright, D. J. *The Apothecary's Shop: Essays on Literature.* Philadelphia: Dufour Editions, 1957.

Fraser, G. S. *The Modern Writer and His World.* London: Derek Verschoyle, 1953.

Furbank, P. N., and R. J. M. Haskell. "The Art of Fiction." *Paris Review* I (Spring 1953), 29–41. An interview with E. M. Forster.

Fussel, Paul, Jr. "E. M. Forster's Mrs. Moore: Some Suggestions." *Philological Quarterly* XXXII (October 1953), 388–95.

Gilomen, W. "Fantasy and Prophecy in E. M. Forster's Work." *English Studies* XXVII (August 1946), 97–112.

The Gospel of Sri Ramakrishna. Translated by Swami Nikhilananda. New York: Ramakrishna-Vivekananda Center, 1958.

Grandsen, K. W. *E. M. Forster.* New York: Grove Press, 1962.

Hafiz of Shiraz. Translated by Peter Avery and John Heath-Stubbs. London: John Murray, 1952.

Hale, Nancy. "A Passage to Relationship." *Antioch Review* XX (Spring 1960), 19–30.

Hall, James. *The Tragic Comedians*. Bloomington: Indiana University Press, 1963.

Hamill, Elizabeth. *These Modern Writers*. Melbourne: Georgian House, 1946.

Hampshire, Stuart. "Two Cheers for Mr. Forster." *The New York Review of Books* VI (May 12, 1966), 14–16.

Hardy, Barbara. *The Appropriate Form: An Essay on the Novel*. London: Athlone Press, University of London, 1964.

Harrison, Gilbert A. "The Modern Mr. Forster." *New Republic* CL (January 11, 1964), 15–16.

Harrison, R. L. "The Manuscript of *A Passage to India*." Ph.D. dissertation, University of Texas, 1964.

Havell, E. B. *A Handbook of Indian Art*. London: John Murray, 1920.

Hoare, Dorothy M. *Some Studies in the Modern Novel*. Philadelphia: Dufour Editions, 1953.

Hoggart, Richard. "The Unsuspected Audience." *New Statesman* LVI (September 6, 1958), 308–10.

Hollingsworth, Keith. "*A Passage to India*: The Echoes in the Marabar Caves." *Criticism* IV (Summer 1962), 210–24.

Holt, Lee Elbert. "E. M. Forster and Samuel Butler." *PMLA* LXI (September 1946), 804–19.

Horne, E. A. "Mr. Forster's *A Passage to India*." *New Statesman* XXIII (August 16, 1924), 543–44.

Horowitz, Ellin. "The Communal Ritual and the Dying God in E. M. Forster's *A Passage to India*." *Criticism* VI (Winter 1964), 70–88.

Houlton, Sir John. *Bihar: The Heart of India*. Bombay: Orient Longmans, 1949.

Howe, Susanne. *Novels of Empire*. New York: Columbia University Press, 1949.

Hynes, Samuel. "The Old Man at King's." *Commonweal* LXXIX (February 21, 1964), 635–38.

Johnstone, J. K. *The Bloomsbury Group*. New York: Noonday Press, 1963.

Jones, David. "E. M. Forster on His Life and His Books." *Listener* LXI (January 1, 1959), 11–12.

Kain, Richard M. "Vision and Discovery in E. M. Forster's

A Passage to India." In *Twelve Original Essays on Great English Novels,* edited by Charles Shapiro. Detroit: Wayne State University Press, 1960.

Keir, W. A. S. "*A Passage to India* Reconsidered." *Cambridge Journal* V (April 1952), 426–35.

Kermode, Frank. "Mr. E. M. Forster As a Symbolist." In *Forster: A Collection of Critical Essays,* edited by Malcolm Bradbury. Englewood Cliffs, N.J.: Prentice-Hall, 1966.

Kettle, Arnold. *An Introduction to the English Novel.* 2 vols. London: Hutchinson's Universal Library, 1953.

Kirkpatrick, B. J. *A Bibliography of E. M. Forster.* London: Rupert Hart-Davis, 1965.

Leach, Elsie. "Forster's *A Passage to India.*" *Explicator* XIII (October 1954), 13.

Leavis, F. R. "E. M. Forster." *Scrutiny* VII (September 1938).

Leavis, F. R. *The Common Pursuit.* London: Chatto & Windus, 1952.

Leavis, Q. D. *Fiction and the Reading Public.* London: Chatto & Windus, 1932.

The Letters of T. E. Lawrence. Edited by David Garnett. London: Jonathan Cape, 1938.

Lunan, N. M. "The Novels of E. M. Forster." *Durham University Journal* XXXVI (March 1945), 52–57.

Macaulay, Rose. *The Writings of E. M. Forster.* New York: Harcourt, Brace & Co., 1938.

MacDonald, Alastair. "Class-Consciousness in E. M. Forster." *University of Kansas City Review* XXVII (Spring 1961), 235–40.

Maclean, Hugh. "The Structure of *A Passage to India.*" *University of Toronto Quarterly* XXII (January 1953), 157–71.

McConkey, James. *The Novels of E. M. Forster.* Ithaca, N.Y.: Cornell University Press, 1957.

McCormick, John. *Catastrophe and Imagination.* London: Longmans, Green & Co., 1957.

McDowell, Frederick P. W. "The Newest Elucidations of Forster." *English Fiction in Transition* V (1962), 51–58.

McLuhan, Herbert Marshall. "Kipling and Forster." *Sewanee Review* LII (Summer 1944), 332–43.

Moore, Harry T. *E. M. Forster*. Columbia Essays on Modern Writers Series. New York: Columbia University Press, 1965.

Natwar-Singh, K., ed. *E. M. Forster: A Tribute*. New York: Harcourt, Brace & World, 1964.

Nierenberg, Edwin. "The Withered Priestess: Mrs. Moore's Incomplete Passage to India." *Modern Language Quarterly* XXV (June 1964), 198–204.

O'Connor, William Van. "A Visit with E. M. Forster." *Western Review* XIX (Spring 1955), 215–19.

Oliver, H. J. *The Art of E. M. Forster*. Melbourne: Melbourne University Press, 1960.

Panter-Downes, Mollie. "Profiles: Kingsman." *New Yorker* XXXV (September 19, 1959), 51–80.

Parry, Benita. "Passage to More than India." In *Forster: A Collection of Critical Essays*, edited by Malcolm Bradbury. Englewood Cliffs, N.J.: Prentice-Hall, 1966.

Pedersen, Glen. "Forster's Symbolic Form." *Kenyon Review* XXXI (Spring 1959), 231–49.

Poems from Iqbal. Translated by V. G. Kiernan. London: John Murray, 1955.

Pritchett, V. S. "Mr. Forster's New Year." *New Statesman* LVI (December 21, 1958), 912–13.

Ransom, J. C. "E. M. Forster." *Kenyon Review* V (Autumn 1943), 618–23.

Rao, Raja. "Recollections of E. M. Forster." In *E. M. Forster: A Tribute*, edited by K. Natwar-Singh. New York: Harcourt, Brace & World, 1964.

Rau, Santha Rama. Introduction to "Indian Entries from a Diary," by E. M. Forster. *Harper's* CCXXIV (February 1962).

Reid, Forrest. *Private Road*. London: Faber & Faber, 1940.

Richards, I. A. "A Passage to Forster." *Forum* LXXVIII (December 1927), 914-20.

Routh, H. V. *English Literature and Ideas in the Twentieth Century*. London: Methuen & Co., 1946.

Savage, D. S. *The Withered Branch*. London: Eyre & Spottiswoode, 1950.

Shahane, V. A. "Symbolism in E. M. Forster's *A Passage to India*: 'Temple.'" *English Studies* XLIV (December 1963), 423–31.

Shanks, Edward. "Mr. E. M. Forster." *London Mercury* XVI (July 1927), 265–74.

Sharif, Ja'Far. *Islam in India*. Translated by G. A. Herklots. rev. ed. by William Crooke. London: Oxford University Press, 1921.

Sharma, Sri Ram. *The Religious Policy of the Mughal Emperors*. 2nd ed. New York: Asia Publishing House, 1962.

Shusterman, David. "The Curious Case of Professor Godbole: *A Passage to India* Reexamined." *PMLA* (September 1961), 426–35.

The Song of God: Bhagavad-Gita. Translated by Swami Prabhavananda and Christopher Isherwood. New York: New American Library, 1954.

Spence, Jonathan. "E. M. Forster at Eighty." *New Republic* CXLI (October 5, 1959), 17–21.

Stone, Wilfred. *The Cave and the Mountain*. Stanford, Calif.: Stanford University Press, 1966.

Stonier, G. W. "Books in General." *New Statesman and Nation* XXIV (November 1942), 341.

Swinnerton, Frank. *The Georgian Literary Scene*. London: Hutchinson & Co., 1939.

Thomson, George H. "Thematic Symbol in *A Passage to India*." *Twentieth Century Literature* VII (July 1961), 51–63.

Trilling, Lionel. *E. M. Forster*. New York: New Directions, 1943.

The Vishnu Purana: A System of Hindu Mythology and Tradition. Translated by H. H. Wilson. 6 vols. London, 1864.

Voorhees, Richard J. "The Novels of E. M. Forster." *South Atlantic Quarterly* LIII (January 1954), 89–99.

Warner, Rex. *E. M. Forster*. British Writers and their Work Series. London: Longmans, Green & Co., 1950.

White, Gertrude M. "*A Passage to India*: Analysis and Revaluation." *PMLA* LXVIII (September 1953), 641–57.

Wilde, Alan. *Art and Order: A Study of E. M. Forster*. New York: New York University Press, 1964.

Wilson, Angus. "A Conversation with E. M. Forster." *Encounter* IX (November 1957), 52–57.

Woolf, Virginia. "The Novels of E. M. Forster." *Atlantic Monthly* CXL (November 1927), 642–48.

Zabel, Morton Dauwen. *Craft and Character in Modern Fiction.* New York: Viking Press, 1957.

Zimmer, Heinrich. *Philosophies of India.* Edited by Joseph Campbell. Cleveland: World Publishing Co., 1956.

Zwerdling, Alex. "The Novels of E. M. Forster." *Twentieth Century Literature* II (January 1957), 171–81.

Index

Ackerley, J. R., 24, 27, 29n, 31–34n, 44, 65, 67, 68n
Akbar, 20, 22
Alamgir (Aurangzebe), 21, 22, 40, 63n
Alexandria: A History and a Guide, 11
Allen, Glen O., 122, 130–32, 138–40, 147, 149n, 154, 158
Allen, Walter, 124
Apostles, 4
Appearances, 67, 72
Archetypes and the Collective Unconscious, The, 140
Arctic Summer, 9
Asoka, 20, 21, 73
Aspects of the Novel, 4
Atman, 138, 139, 144, 180n
Aurangabad, 41–45, 50
Aziz, Dr., 21, 29, 30, 32n, 34, 39, 43–46, 48, 50, 52–57, 60, 63n, 72, 79–82, 84–88, 90–97, 101, 103–5, 107, 112, 115, 118, 125, 126, 129, 130, 132, 141, 142, 144–47, 156, 159, 160, 162, 166, 175, 176, 178, 181–83, 186–90

Babur, 21
Beer, J. B., 135, 157
Bentley, Phyllis, 112
Bhagavad Gita, 61
Bhagavata Purana, 61, 62, 181
Bihar, 20
Bloomsbury Group, 4
Boyle, Ted, 155

Bradbury, Malcolm, 119–21
Brahma, 153, 172n
Brahman, 138, 139, 144, 148, 151, 153, 166, 172n, 181, 186
Brower, Reuben, 127, 129, 143
Brown, E. K., 122, 128, 129, 142, 143, 150, 155, 158, 161
Bundelkand, 136

Cambridge, 3, 4, 7, 8, 12, 30, 124
Cecil, David, 134, 161
Celestial Omnibus, The, 11
Chandrapore, 20, 29, 34, 43, 82, 85, 90, 97, 106, 113, 118, 134, 167, 189
Chaudhuri, Nirad C., 115, 116, 118
Chhatarpur, 32, 48, 61, 64, 65, 67
Chirol, Sir Valentine, 23–25, 28, 30, 34, 35, 37, 38, 40n, 176n
Crews, Frederick, 12, 117, 144, 145, 161

Dauner, Louise, 140
Davis, F. Hadland, 55
Devi, 170
Dewas Senior, 3, 32n, 34, 37–41, 57, 62
Dickenson, G. Lowes, 10, 12, 31, 33, 65, 67, 70, 72, 111, 124, 162, 183n, 186
Divani Shamsi Tabriz (Rumi), 54

Eapen, Karippacheril Chakko, 145, 149n